HUMAN BODY

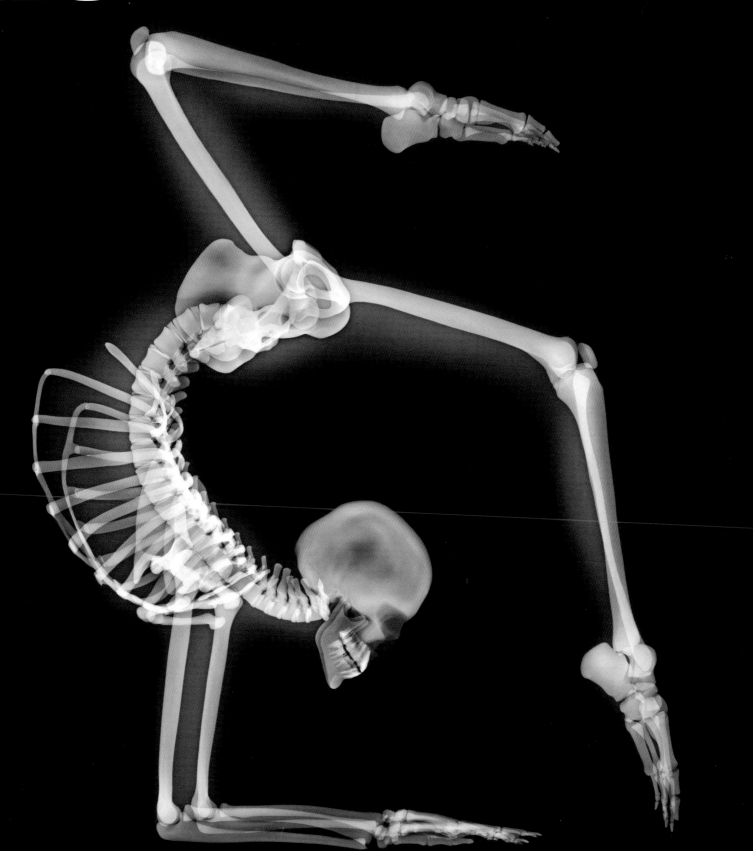

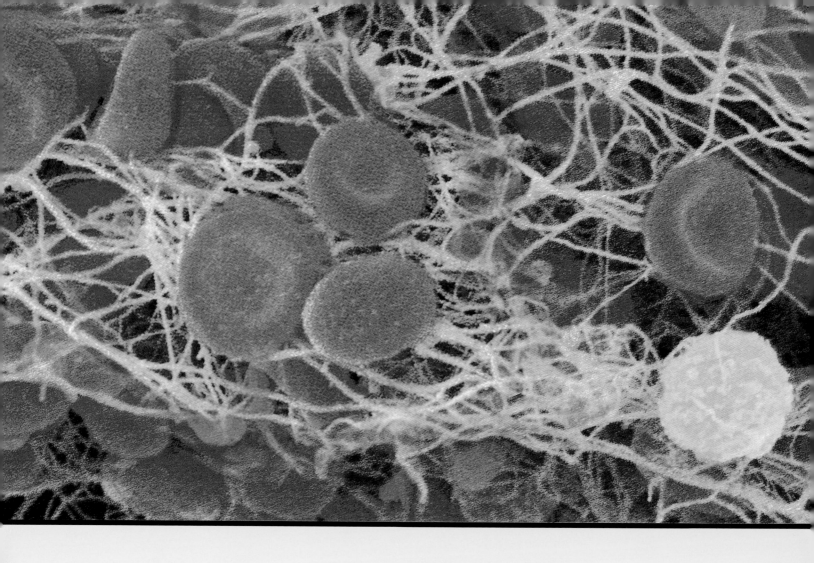

HUMA

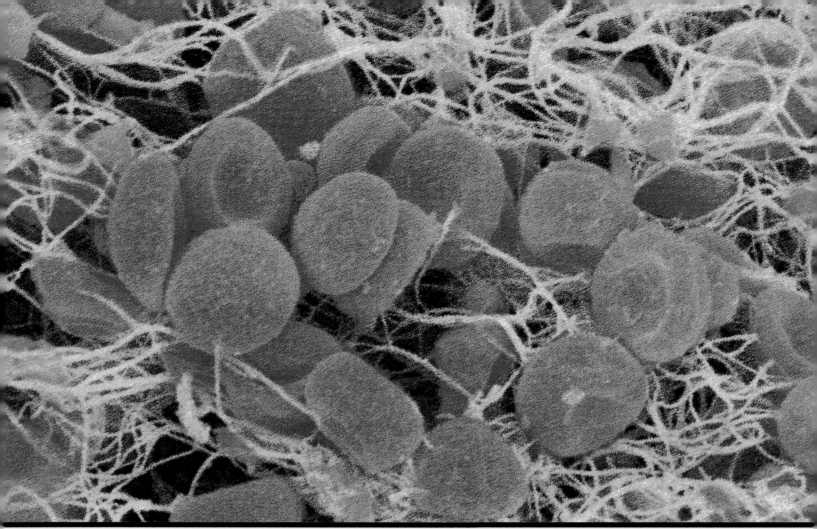

YOUR BODY CONTAINS ABOUT 25 TRILLION RED BLOOD CELLS BUT ONLY ABOUT 35 BILLION WHITE BLOOD CELLS.

N BODY

STEVE SETFORD

SCHOLASTIC discover more™

Be a Brainiac digital book

Your brain is the world's best supercomputer! It controls your thoughts, memories, emotions, and dreams. And it can develop and change. Your digital book is full of things to do to give your brainpower a big boost.

Your digital book is very simple to use. Enter the code (bottom right) to download it to any Mac or PC. Open it in Adobe Reader, also free to download. Then you're all set!

BE A BRAINIAC

A digital companion to **Human Bo**

Improve your short-term memory

Thousands of times a day, you need to remember something for just a few seconds. The part of the brain most used for short-term memory is called the prefrontal lobe. Give this part of your brain a great workout!

Remembering lists
Do you sometimes struggle to remember random collections of facts? (Like what homework you have this week!) This game will help you.

Remembering numbers
Most people can hold only about 7 pieces of information in their minds at a time. See if you can do better.

Look at these 16 numbers for 45 seconds and try to remember them in the right order.
Tip: Divide the numbers into several smaller groups.
Now click on the numbers.

5 8 3 9 1 6 5 2 0 7 3 4 9 6 1 2

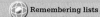

Scoring
Remembering lists: Score 1 point for every object remembered (maximum 20 points)
Remembering numbers: Score 1 point for each number remembered in the right order (maximum 16 points)
Total: 36
A score of 30 or more means you have a great short-term memory. If you scored less, don't worry! Read on for more ways to improve your memory.

🔍 **discover more** – improve your long-term memory   ⊕ Remembering lists

Memory test
Your digital book is packed with fun games and quizzes to help improve your memory and attention.

Every time you have a new thought or form a memory, you create a connection in your brain

Remembering lists

Here's a great way to remember lists. The journey method dates back to the ancient Greeks and Romans. They used loci ("places" in Latin) to help them remember important things in speeches in the right order. Today, Dominic O'Brien has used the journey method to win the World Memory Championships eight times and earn a place in the Guinness Book of World Records.

The journey method
Associate each word on a list with something you see on a route you take often (such as around your house or the way to school). Then build a story about these things. In this example, you can remember a shopping list using things you see on an imaginary walk around town.

Shopping list
- water gun
- apples
- pet food
- sweets
- football
- comic book
- Halloween costume

You need to remember the 7 items on this shopping list.

1. Rain is falling (this reminds you of the water gun)
2. You see a red hat (the apples)
3. There's a cat running itself on a wall (the pet food)
4. You pass a line of cars (the brightly coloured sweets)
5. You see a round traffic sign (the football)
6. Your friends are laughing at a joke (the comic book)
7. You walk under the autumn leaves (the Halloween costume)

Top 10 tips for a healthy memory

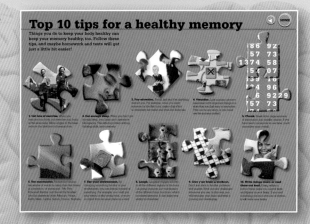

Top 10 tips for a healthy memory

Train your brain
Learn simple techniques, based on your everyday experiences, to make a more brainsmart you!

Fit and healthy
Just like the rest of your body, your brain needs to stay healthy. Your digital book is full of tips on how to look after it.

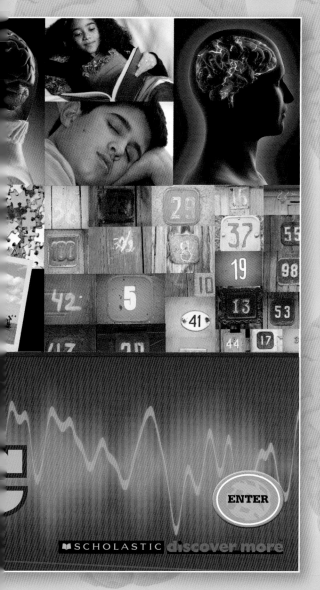

ENTER

SCHOLASTIC discover more

Consultant: Peter Ellis, Senior Lecturer, Faculty of Health and Social Care, Canterbury Christ Church University, Kent, UK
Project Editor: Andrea Bagg
Project Art Editors: Emma Forge, Tom Forge
Art Director: Bryn Walls
Managing Editor: Miranda Smith
Managing Production Editor: Stephanie Engel
Cover Designer: Neal Cobourne
DTP: John Goldsmid

> "The human foot is a masterpiece of engineering and a work of art."
> —LEONARDO DA VINCI (1452–1519), ARTIST, INVENTOR, AND ANATOMIST

Library of Congress Cataloging-in-Publication Data Available
Distributed in the UK by Scholastic UK Ltd, Westfield Road, Southam, Warwickshire, England CV47 0RA

ISBN 978-1-407-14250-0

10 9 8 7 6 5 4 3 2 1   14 15 16 17 18

Printed in Singapore   46
First edition, July 2014

Scholastic is constantly working to lessen the environmental impact of our manufacturing processes. To view our industry-leading paper procurement policy, visit www.scholastic.com/paperpolicy.

TASTE BUDS ON THE SURFACE OF THE TONGUE

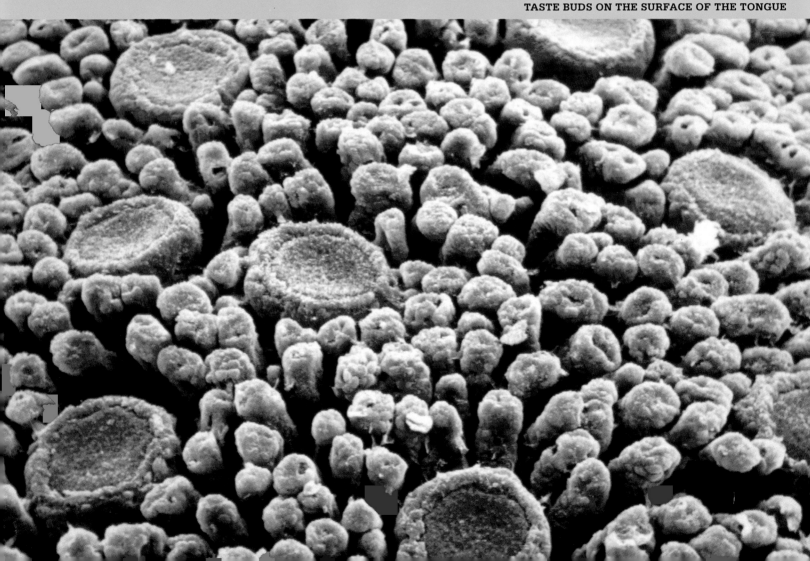

Contents

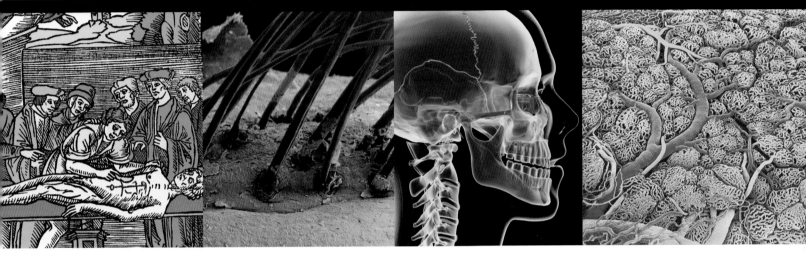

Paralympian

Your body can help you do anything. In 2006, Vanessa Low of Germany lost her lower legs in an accident. However, with rigorous training, she built up her thigh muscles. Using artificial limbs called blades, she has become a medal-winning long jumper. Here, she competes in the women's long jump final at the 2012 Paralympics in London.

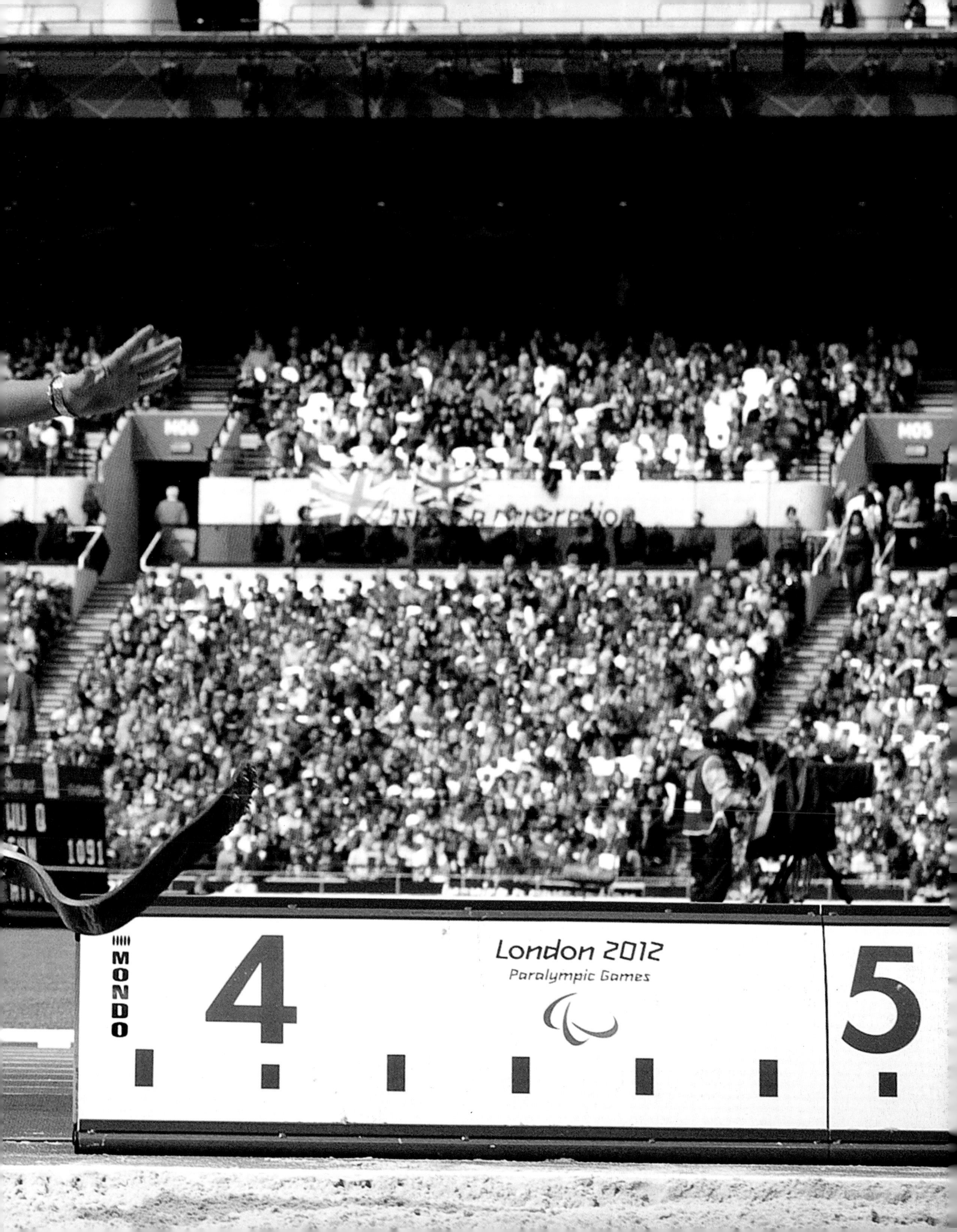

MONDO
4
London 2012
Paralympic Games
5

Star pupil

The iris looks like a starburst around the eye's dark pupil. Its muscle fibres adjust to change the amount of light that enters the eye. They contract, or shrink, the pupil in bright light. They enlarge the pupil when it is darker. The coloured patterns of your irises are unique to you, just as your fingerprints are.

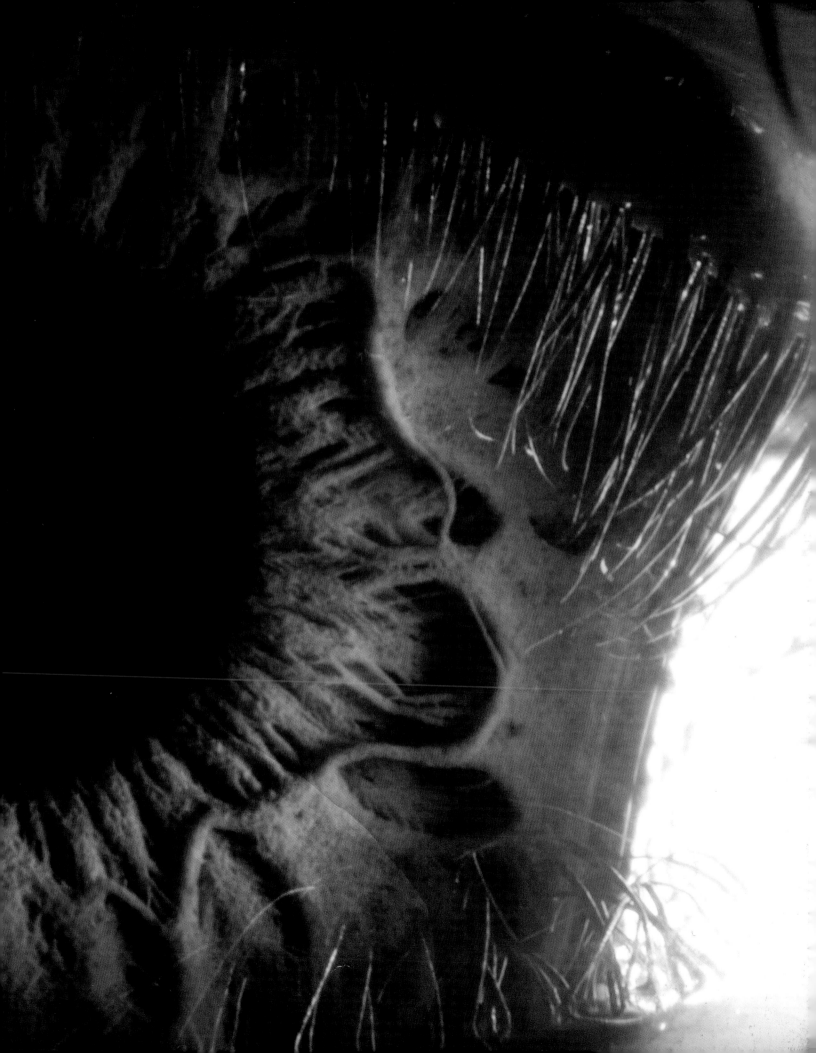

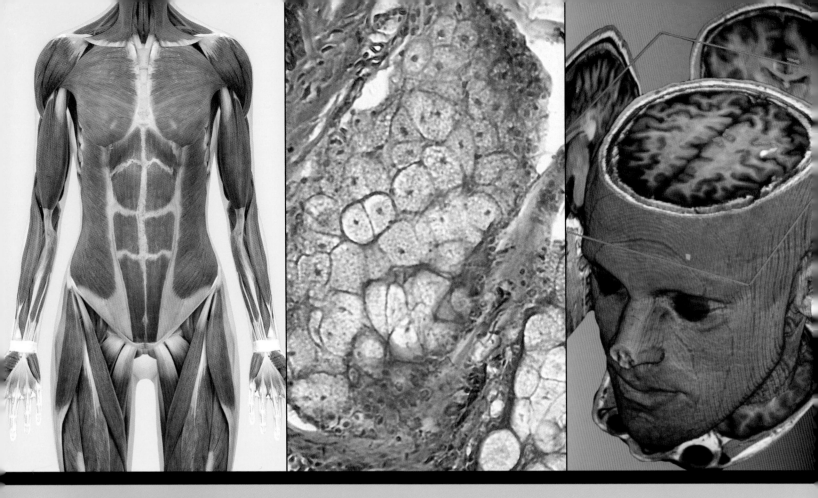

Your amazing
bo

* What is a body system?

* Which tiny part of your body makes energy?

* How do doctors use magnets to see inside your body?

If you wanted to build yourself from scratch, piece by piece, you'd have to start with unimaginably small particles of matter called atoms. The ways that these atoms link together to form so many different structures make your body totally amazing.

Atoms
Inside atoms are even smaller particles. Protons (green) and neutrons (red) are surrounded by shooting electrons.

Molecules
When two or more atoms join together, they make a molecule.

Macromolecules
Groups of molecules join together to form macromolecules. These contain hundreds or thousands of atoms. They are found in cells.

Cells
Cells are the smallest units of life. They hold everything necessary to keep you alive. This is a heart muscle cell.

Tissues
Cells of the same type, grouped together, form tissue. Here, densely packed heart muscle cells form cardiac tissue.

Organs
Organs are made up of more than one kind of tissue. The heart is made up mainly of cardiac muscle tissue and connective tissue.

Body systems
Organs and body parts work together in systems. In the cardiovascular system, the heart pumps blood around the body.

Whole body
The cardiovascular system is just one of your body systems (see pages 18–19). The systems all work together to keep you healthy.

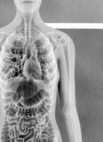

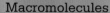

There are approximately

7000,000,000,
000,000,000,
,000,000,000
(7 billion billion billion)
atoms in the body of an
average-size adult

Cell wall

Channel

Nucleus

Life-giving cell
All living things are made up of cells
(see pages 26–27). Your body is made
of about 50 trillion of them! Here you
can see a cell's nucleus (its control
centre), and channels in its outside
wall that help nutrients and other
substances pass into the cell.

Body parts [Bigger bits]

You are incredibly complex, crammed with more than 7,500 parts. Some of these are tissues, and others are organs or parts of organs (see page 14). The skin is the largest organ, weighing about 4 kg (9 lbs) in an average man. The "greediest" organ is the brain, which consumes 25 percent of the body's energy and 20 percent of the oxygen taken in by breathing. Whatever its size or importance, every single part belongs to one of the body's major systems (see pages 18–19).

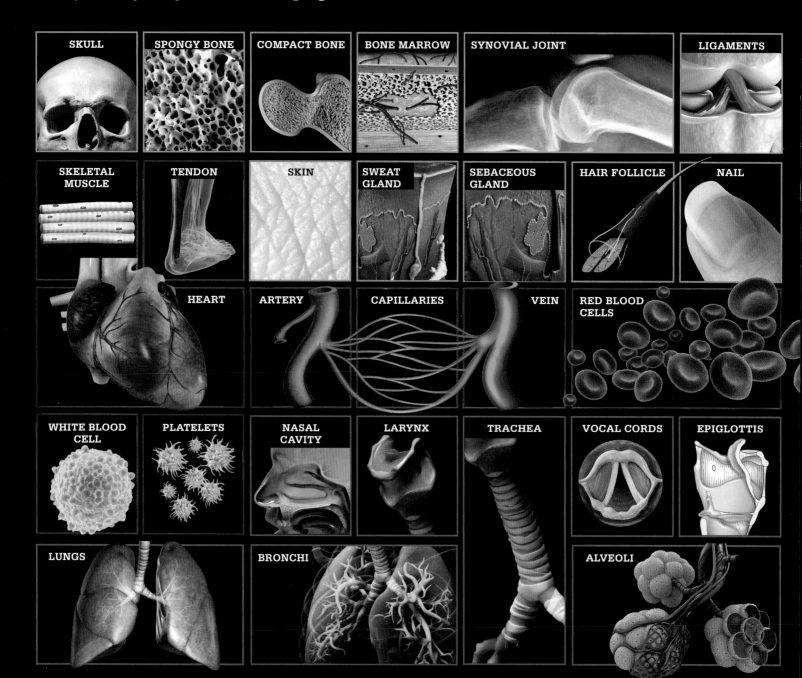

SKULL

SPONGY BONE

COMPACT BONE

BONE MARROW

SYNOVIAL JOINT

LIGAMENTS

SKELETAL MUSCLE

TENDON

SKIN

SWEAT GLAND

SEBACEOUS GLAND

HAIR FOLLICLE

NAIL

HEART

ARTERY

CAPILLARIES

VEIN

RED BLOOD CELLS

WHITE BLOOD CELL

PLATELETS

NASAL CAVITY

LARYNX

TRACHEA

VOCAL CORDS

EPIGLOTTIS

LUNGS

BRONCHI

ALVEOLI

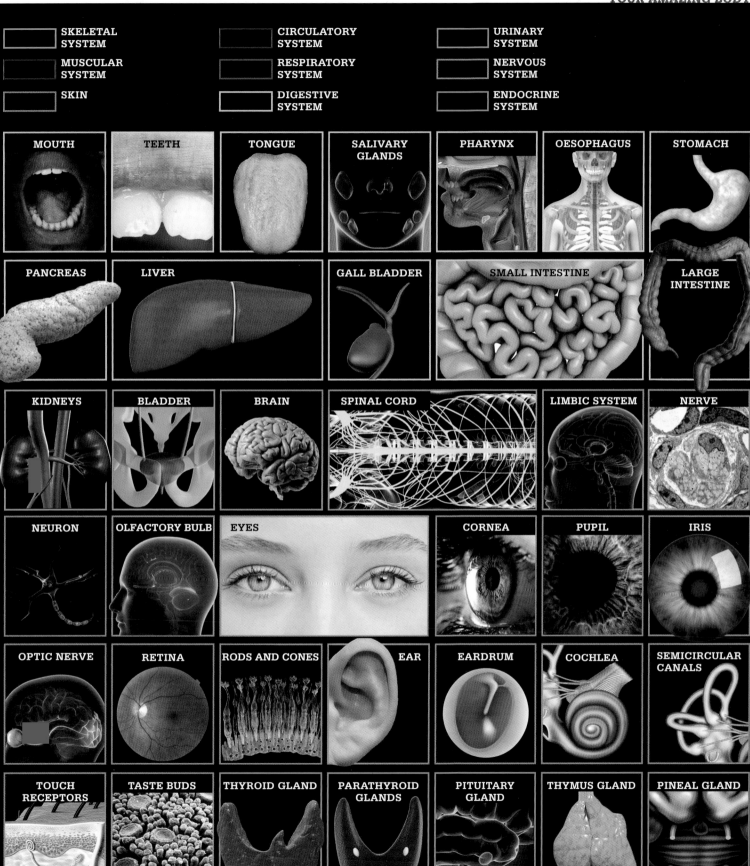

SKELETAL SYSTEM

MUSCULAR SYSTEM

SKIN

CIRCULATORY SYSTEM

RESPIRATORY SYSTEM

DIGESTIVE SYSTEM

URINARY SYSTEM

NERVOUS SYSTEM

ENDOCRINE SYSTEM

MOUTH

TEETH

TONGUE

SALIVARY GLANDS

PHARYNX

OESOPHAGUS

STOMACH

PANCREAS

LIVER

GALL BLADDER

SMALL INTESTINE

LARGE INTESTINE

KIDNEYS

BLADDER

BRAIN

SPINAL CORD

LIMBIC SYSTEM

NERVE

NEURON

OLFACTORY BULB

EYES

CORNEA

PUPIL

IRIS

OPTIC NERVE

RETINA

RODS AND CONES

EAR

EARDRUM

COCHLEA

SEMICIRCULAR CANALS

TOUCH RECEPTORS

TASTE BUDS

THYROID GLAND

PARATHYROID GLANDS

PITUITARY GLAND

THYMUS GLAND

PINEAL GLAND

Body systems [Jobs to do]

Life would be difficult if you had to stop breathing to digest a meal! Luckily, your body can do lots of things at the same time. That's because it has separate body systems to handle different tasks.

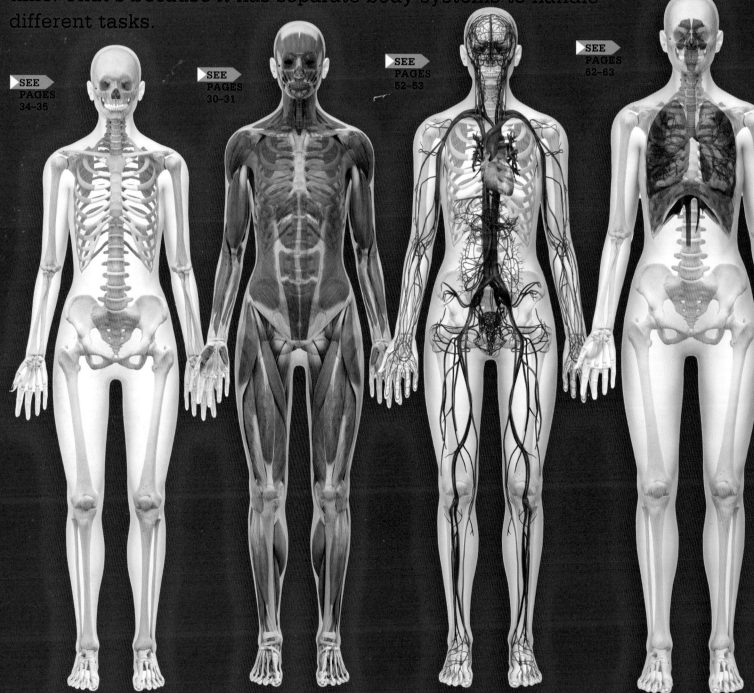

SEE PAGES 34–35

SEE PAGES 30–31

SEE PAGES 52–53

SEE PAGES 62–63

Skeletal
Your bones keep you from collapsing in a heap! They're joined by ligaments and tendons. Your skeletal system makes up about 14 percent of your total weight.

Muscular
You can't move without muscles! They also power activities such as breathing. You are born with all the muscle fibres you'll ever have. As you get stronger, they grow thicker.

Circulatory
Your heart pumps blood around a transport system to supply cells with oxygen, nutrients, and energy. The only part of you with no blood supply is your cornea, at the front of your eye.

Respiratory
Your lungs and airways bring fresh oxygen into your body and expel carbon dioxide. Before you were born, your lungs were full of fluid. They filled up with air a few seconds after your birth.

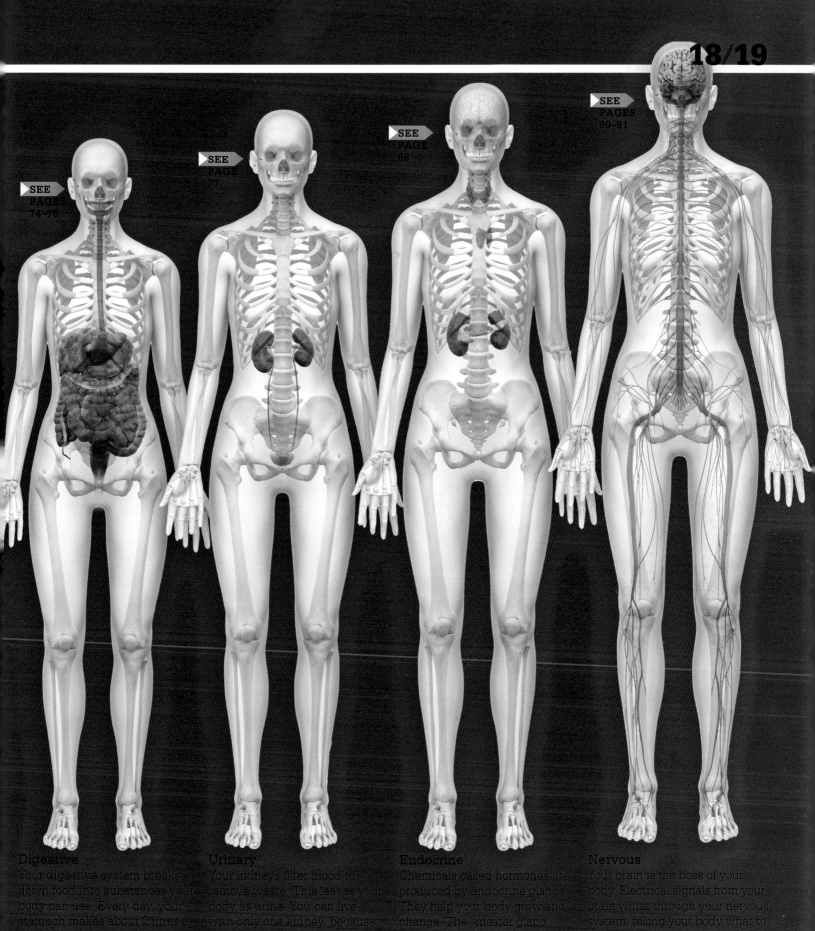

SEE PAGES 74-75

SEE PAGE 77

SEE PAGE 88

SEE PAGES 80-81

Digestive
Your digestive system breaks down food into substances your body can use. Every day, your stomach makes about 2 litres (4 pints) of acid, which helps kill bacteria and aids digestion.

Urinary
Your kidneys filter blood to remove waste. This leaves your body as urine. You can live with only one kidney, because it can adjust to filter twice as much blood as before.

Endocrine
Chemicals called hormones are produced by endocrine glands. They help your body grow and change. The "master gland" is the pea-size pituitary – its hormones control other glands.

Nervous
Your brain is the boss of your body. Electrical signals from your brain whizz through your nervous system, telling your body what to do. Your brain gets 20 percent of your body's total blood supply!

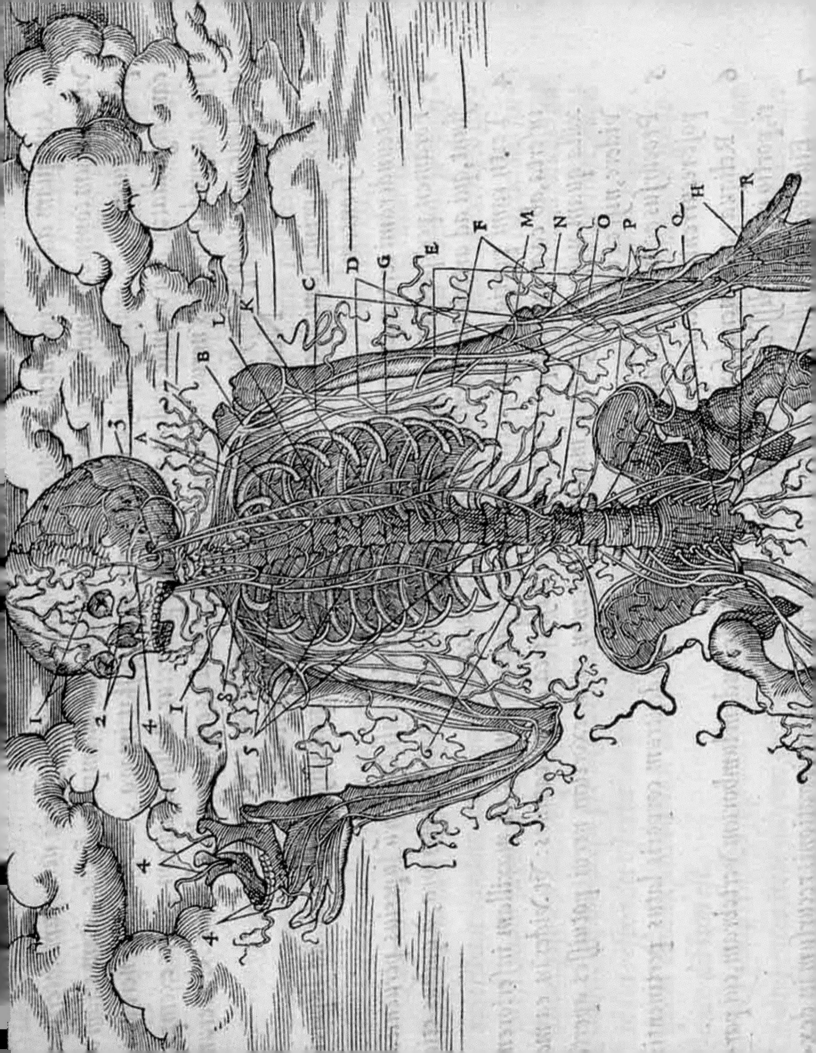

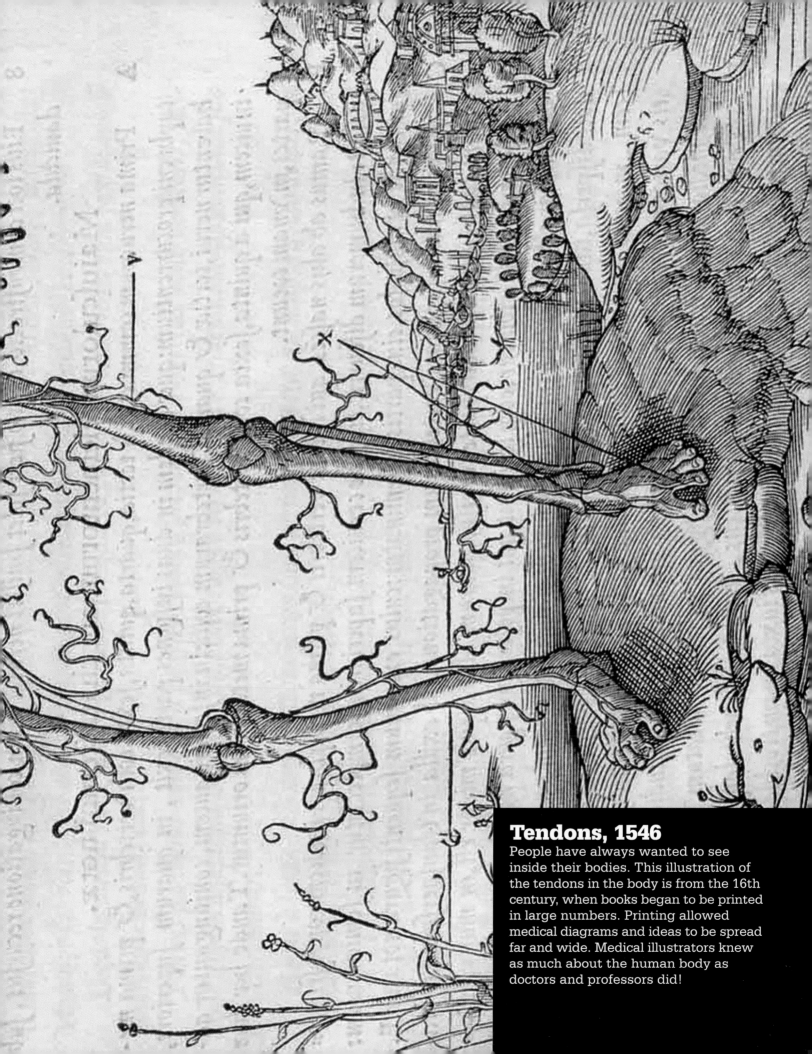

Tendons, 1546

People have always wanted to see inside their bodies. This illustration of the tendons in the body is from the 16th century, when books began to be printed in large numbers. Printing allowed medical diagrams and ideas to be spread far and wide. Medical illustrators knew as much about the human body as doctors and professors did!

Taking a look [Body study]

At one time, the only way to see under the surface of the body was to dissect, or cut up, a corpse. Today's high-tech devices can see inside living bodies without making a single cut.

First look

Ancient Egyptians learned about human anatomy when they removed organs before mummifying the dead. Later, ancient Greek doctors dissected human and animal corpses to investigate the body's workings.

First medieval dissection

In 1315, Mondino de' Luzzi performed the first official human dissection in medieval Europe. Bans had prevented such dissections since about 200 CE.

Making bigger

In the 17th century, the invention of the microscope enabled many small body structures, bacteria, and viruses to be studied for the first time. Electron microscopes, developed in 1933, show even more detail.

Old microscope

Two lenses inside a tube create an enlarged image of a sample mounted on a glass slide.

Slides

Microscopic view of heart muscle

Under the surface

This 18th-century drawing shows the arteries of the face. It was based on what doctors had learned by cutting up bodies.

Body snatchers

In Europe and America during the 18th and 19th centuries, graves were often robbed to supply doctors in medical schools with bodies to dissect.

Electron microscope view

An electron microscope magnifies using a beam of electrically charged particles called electrons. Here, nasal hairs and bacteria (yellow) are enlarged 7,000 times.

50 million times

X-rays

Discovered in 1895 by Wilhelm Röntgen, X-rays can be passed through the body to create images. Computed tomography (CT), invented in 1971, uses a computer to build images as a scanner moves around the body, firing X-rays at it.

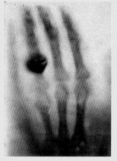

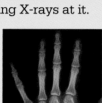

First-ever X-ray
This X-ray image shows the hand of Anna Röntgen, Wilhelm's wife. Her wedding ring is clearly visible.

Modern X-ray
X-rays are blocked by dense body parts. Bones and teeth show up as white on a dark background.

In three dimensions

Technology can now give us 3D views into the body. Ultrasound scanners form images by sending sound waves into the body. Magnetic resonance imaging (MRI) forms images using magnets and radio waves aimed into the body.

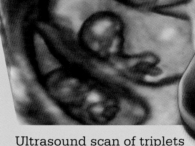

Ultrasound scan of triplets
An ultrasound scanner beams high-frequency sound waves at the body. It analyzes the echoes that bounce back off internal structures and organs.

Ligament CT scan
CT scans show soft tissue better than ordinary X-ray images do. This scan shows damage to a knee ligament (dark purple).

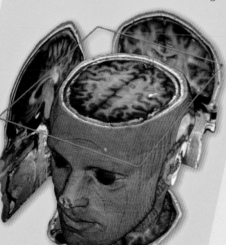

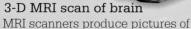

3-D MRI scan of brain
MRI scanners produce pictures of "slices" through different body organs and structures. These slices can be stacked together to make 3D views.

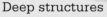

Deep structures
MRI scans can make images of any part of the body, from almost any angle. In this scan of the head, you can see the top of the cerebrum (see pages 86–87), the nasal cavity, and the tongue.

Your body is made up of about 60 simple substances called elements. To operate smoothly, it needs around 27 of them. Of these 27, only 6 make up almost all of your weight. Hydrogen and oxygen, 2 of the 6, combine readily and are found in your body mainly as water. In fact, you are mostly water!

"Big six" elements

Just six elements make up 98.5 percent of your body's weight. They are oxygen, carbon, hydrogen, nitrogen, calcium, and phosphorus. Oxygen is by far the largest component, followed by carbon, which is present in all your body's structures.

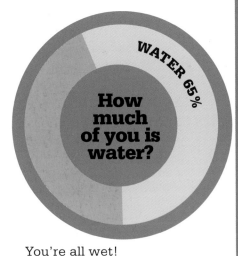

WATER 65%

How much of you is water?

You're all wet!
You may feel pretty solid, but nearly two-thirds of your body is water!

Why should I drink lots of water?
You lose water when you go to the bathroom, sweat, or breathe out. A nine-year-old child, for example, loses around 1.5 litres (3 pints), or 7 glasses, of water a day. If you don't drink water to replace what you've lost, your body will not work properly.

Your body is worth $160
in terms of the elements it contains

Oxygen
Most of the oxygen in your body is combined with hydrogen as water. You also take in oxygen from the air you breathe and use it to help make fuel for your body.

WATER

65 percent

Carbon
A diamond is pure carbon. There are no diamonds inside your body, but there is still an awful lot of carbon! There is carbon in all your body tissues.

DIAMOND

18 percent

Hydrogen
Hydrogen gas was once used in airships, but it catches fire easily and caused accidents. Your own hydrogen is safely locked up in water – so you won't ignite!

AIRSHIP

10 percent

Nitrogen
Many body chemicals, including the enzymes that help you digest food, contain nitrogen. Liquid nitrogen is very cold and is used to quick-freeze food.

LIQUID NITROGEN

3 percent

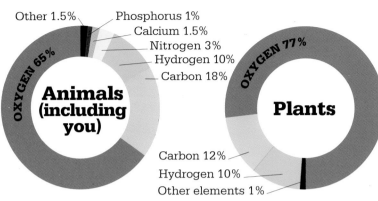

Other 1.5%
Phosphorus 1%
Calcium 1.5%
Nitrogen 3%
Hydrogen 10%
Carbon 18%
OXYGEN 65%

Animals (including you)

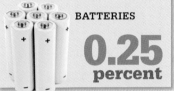

OXYGEN 77%

Plants

Carbon 12%
Hydrogen 10%
Other elements 1%

Animals v. plants!
Like animals, plants are made mostly of oxygen, carbon, and hydrogen. But the amounts differ. One big difference is that there is very little calcium in plants, since they have no bones!

Other elements

In addition to the "big six", your body contains many other elements in very small amounts. They make up the remaining 1.5 percent of your body weight. No matter how tiny the proportions, all these elements play vital roles.

Potassium
Potassium helps your nerve cells send electrical signals. Some batteries use potassium to produce electricity.

BATTERIES

0.25 percent

Magnesium
Magnesium helps your brain and muscles function healthily. It also helps put the *bang* in fireworks!

FIREWORKS

0.05 percent

Sulphur
The yellow mineral sulphur is found in collagen. This protein is in your skin, hair, nails, and other tissues.

NATURAL SULPHUR

0.25 percent

Iron
Iron is used to make red blood cells. It also helps those red blood cells carry oxygen around your body.

RED BLOOD CELL

0.006 percent

Sodium
Sodium affects your blood pressure. It also helps control the amount of water in your body.

SALT (SODIUM CHLORIDE)

0.15 percent

Iodine
Iodine helps your body grow and develop. It is used in medicine to kill germs.

MEDICAL IODINE

0.0004 percent

Chlorine
Chlorine helps keep your body fluids in balance.

0.15 percent

Calcium
This element is a major part of your bones and teeth – it helps keep them hard and strong. It also makes eggshells and seashells hard.

EGGS

1.5 percent

Phosphorus
Flammable phosphorus is used in match heads. It is also found in bones, in teeth, and in DNA (see pages 100–101).

MATCHES

1 percent

And some of the rest . . .

Fluorine	Chromium
Zinc	Manganese
Silicon	Arsenic
Copper	Lithium
Boron	Molybdenum
Selenium	Cobalt
Nickel	Vanadium

Cells [Smallest living units]

Our bodies contain about 50 trillion cells! Cells are the basic living units of the body from which all its tissues and organs are made. They process the food that the body absorbs and turn it into energy. Most cells are incredibly tiny.

Inside a cell

A cell has a control centre, called a nucleus. It also has other structures, called organelles. Each organelle has its own task.

Centriole
This structure helps in cell division.

Cell membrane
This regulates the flow of substances into and out of the cell.

Nucleus
The DNA (see pages 100–101) here contains instructions that tell the cell what to do.

Endoplasmic reticulum
This makes proteins and helps transport materials through the cell.

Your body makes up to 96 million cells every minute
to replace ones that have worn out

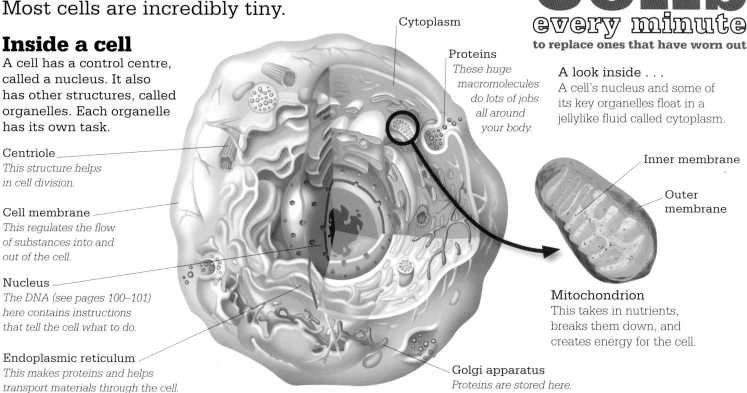

Cytoplasm

Proteins
These huge macromolecules do lots of jobs all around your body.

A look inside . . .
A cell's nucleus and some of its key organelles float in a jellylike fluid called cytoplasm.

Inner membrane

Outer membrane

Mitochondrion
This takes in nutrients, breaks them down, and creates energy for the cell.

Golgi apparatus
Proteins are stored here.

Types of cell

There are about 200 types of cell. Each type has something special to do. Their sizes, shapes, and internal structures depend on their jobs. Nerve cells, for example, have extensions that carry electrical signals.

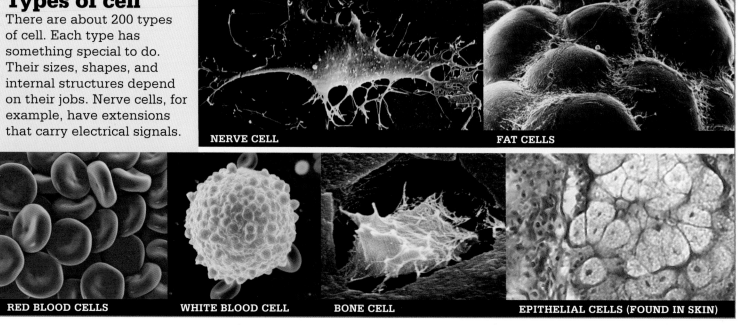

NERVE CELL

FAT CELLS

RED BLOOD CELLS

WHITE BLOOD CELL

BONE CELL

EPITHELIAL CELLS (FOUND IN SKIN)

Cell division

Cells don't last forever, so your body has to make them constantly. New cells are made by mitosis, a process in which an existing cell divides to form a pair of identical "daughter" cells. Mitosis usually takes 30–90 minutes, depending on the type of cell involved.

Rates of cell replacement

Cells that line intestines	3–5 days
Top layer of skin	14–28 days
Entire new skin	28 days
Red blood cells	80–120 days
Liver cells	12 months

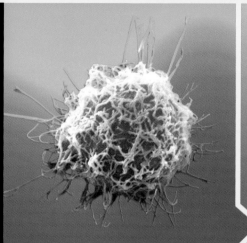

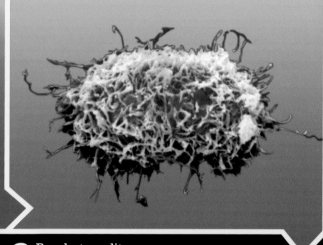

1 Making preparations
Before division starts, the cell makes proteins and new organelles. It also copies its DNA.

2 Ready to split
Inside the cell, the two copies of the DNA are pulled to opposite ends of the cell, forming two new nuclei.

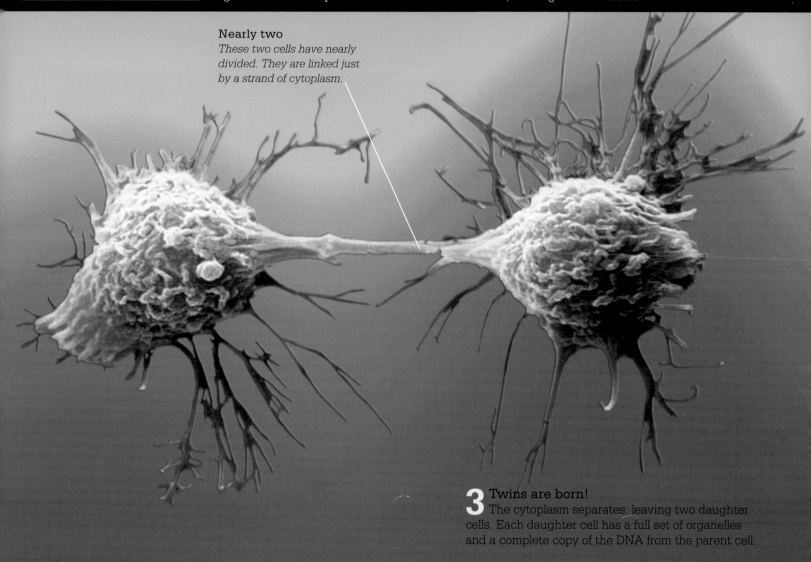

Nearly two
These two cells have nearly divided. They are linked just by a strand of cytoplasm.

3 Twins are born!
The cytoplasm separates, leaving two daughter cells. Each daughter cell has a full set of organelles and a complete copy of the DNA from the parent cell.

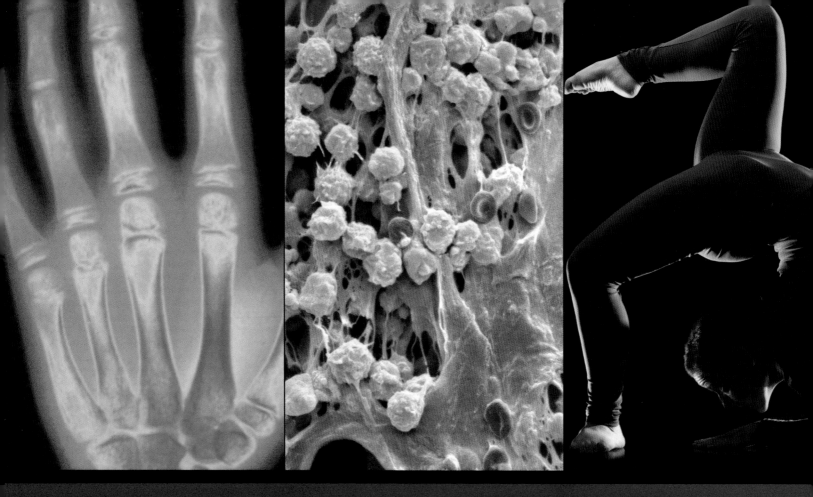

On the
mo

- Why does a baby have more bones than you do?

* What makes millions of blood cells every second?

- How are gymnasts able to bend in half?

ve

Muscles [Body movers]

Muscles make up half the body weight of an average person. The muscles you use when you walk, run, jump, climb, throw a ball, or smile are known as skeletal muscles.

Major skeletal muscles

Your body has over 600 skeletal muscles. Your face alone uses at least 30 muscles to look happy, sad, or surprised. Some skeletal muscles lie close to the surface under your skin; others are deeper. Muscles are attached to bones by strong cords called tendons.

Biceps brachii
You use your biceps to bend your elbow.

Rectus abdominis
This abdominal muscle bends your body forwards.

Flexor carpi radialis
This muscle bends your wrist.

Pectoralis major
Your pectoralis pulls your arm towards your body.

Orbicularis oculi
This muscle closes your eye.

FRONT OF BODY

Tendon

External oblique

BACK OF BODY

Trapezius
Your trapezius pulls back your shoulders and head.

External oblique

Deltoid
This muscle moves your arm out and away from your body.

Triceps brachii
You use your triceps to open your elbow joint and straighten your arm.

Latissimus dorsi
Covering a large area of your back, this muscle pulls your arm downwards and backwards.

Flexor digitorum

Gluteus maximus
This pulls back your thigh to straighten your hip.

Muscle facts

Largest	**Gluteus maximus**
Smallest	**Stapedius (in the ear)**
Strongest (relative to size)	**Tongue**
Most used	**Eye muscles (100,000x per day)**

Muscle types

You have three types of muscle: skeletal, smooth, and cardiac. Skeletal muscles are voluntary – they work only when you want them to. The other muscle types are involuntary – you cannot consciously control them.

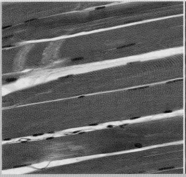

Skeletal muscle
These muscles contract (shorten and fatten) to pull on bones or other tissues to move them. They cannot push.

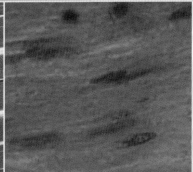

Smooth muscle
This type of muscle pushes food through your digestive system. It is also found in the walls of your airways and blood vessels.

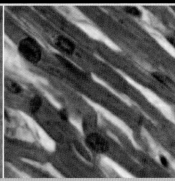

Cardiac muscle
Unlike other muscles, the cardiac muscle never tires. It works non-stop, day and night, to keep your heart pumping.

Quadriceps femoris
This group of four thigh muscles straightens your knee when you walk, run, or kick.

Extensor digitorum longus
This pulls your big toe upwards and turns your foot inwards.

Sartorius

Gastrocnemius
This is your calf muscle. It pulls your foot downwards.

Tibialis anterior
This muscle bends your ankle and pulls your foot upwards.

Soleus

Hamstrings
These three muscles bend your knee joint.

Why do I shiver?
To work properly, your body must stay at a temperature of about 37°C (98.6°F). If you get cold, you shiver – your muscles rapidly tighten and relax. This muscle activity uses a lot of energy, or calories, producing heat as it does so. Your body warms back up again.

Shivering
burns about **400 calories** per hour – roughly the same as swimming laps for an hour

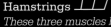

Feeling the cold
Shivering produces heat and helps warm you up.

Muscles in action [Pulling,

If all your muscles pulled in one direction, you could create a force of 23 tonnes. But muscles actually work in teams. When one muscle contracts, another relaxes. This pulls on a bone to move it. The muscles swap roles to move the bone the opposite way.

Kicking a ball

When you decide to kick a ball, your brain sends out an electrical signal. This travels via the neurons of your nervous system (see pages 80–81) to your leg muscles. The signal makes your muscles contract to move your legs.

1 Preparing for the kick
To build up momentum for a powerful kick, you need to pull back your kicking leg, bending it at the knee.

Gluteus maximus contracts
This large muscle contracts to move the hip joint. This pulls back the kicking leg.

Hamstrings contract
The hamstrings contract to bend the knee up.

Quadriceps relax
As the hamstrings contract, the opposing muscles, the quadriceps, relax.

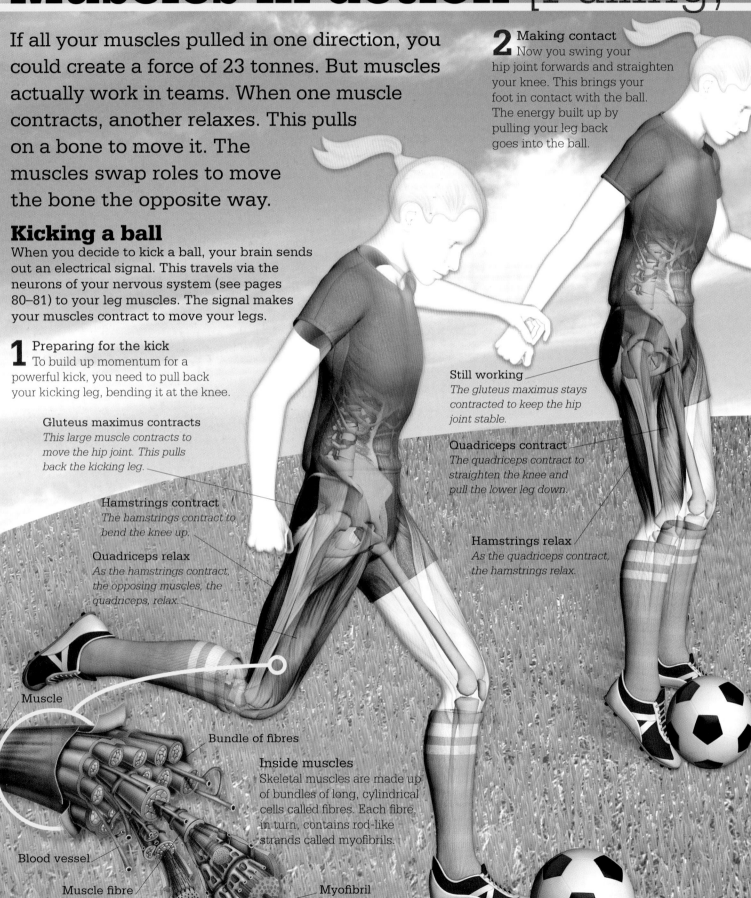

2 Making contact
Now you swing your hip joint forwards and straighten your knee. This brings your foot in contact with the ball. The energy built up by pulling your leg back goes into the ball.

Still working
The gluteus maximus stays contracted to keep the hip joint stable.

Quadriceps contract
The quadriceps contract to straighten the knee and pull the lower leg down.

Hamstrings relax
As the quadriceps contract, the hamstrings relax.

Muscle

Bundle of fibres

Inside muscles
Skeletal muscles are made up of bundles of long, cylindrical cells called fibres. Each fibre, in turn, contains rod-like strands called myofibrils.

Blood vessel

Muscle fibre

Myofibril

not pushing]

Iliopsoas muscle

Iliopsoas muscle
This runs from the lower spine and pelvis to the femur (thigh bone).

Relaxed gluteus
The gluteus maximus relaxes as the hip swings the thigh forwards.

Loose hammies
The hamstrings are relaxed and loose.

3 Following through
Your hip swings your thigh forwards. The iliopsoas muscle provides most of the power for this, and it gives you stability so that you don't fall over as you follow through. It is the partner to the gluteus maximus.

Hip mover
The iliopsoas muscle contracts to pull the femur forwards.

Tight quads
With the knee extended, the quads are now fully contracted.

Weight
The weight is centred on the knee.

Muscles don't push — they only pull

Speed or endurance?
There are two different types of muscle fibre. Fast-twitch fibres are quick to contract but tire rapidly. Slow-twitch fibres contract slowly but keep working for a long time.

Speed
Sprinters have a high proportion of fast-twitch fibres, for short bursts of speed.

Endurance
Marathon runners have more slow-twitch fibres, for long races that need a steady pace.

You do it!
Get a stronger belly
Practise curl-ups to improve the strength of your abdominal muscles.

1 Ask an adult to watch you. Lie on your back on some cushions.

2 Bend your knees. Cross your arms and put your hands on the opposite shoulders. Someone could hold your feet.

3 Curl up to touch your elbows to your thighs.

4 Lower your back to lie down again. That's one curl-up! Now do some more!

Don't do this every day, and don't do it if you're tired or if it hurts!

Without a skeleton, your body would be like a floppy, shapeless beanbag! The bones that make up your skeleton support your body structure and protect your organs. Your bones are growing and changing all the time.

Your two feet contain **52 bones,** about a **quarter** of the bones in your body

Number crunching

Babies have about 300 bones. Adults have 206 bones. You do not lose bones as you get older; rather, many fuse, or join together, as you grow. Bones can be very long, but the smallest bone – the stapes, in your ear – is only 3 mm (0.1 ins), the size of a grain of rice.

Ribs
These flat bones shield the lungs beneath from harm.

Radius (forearm bone)

6 Arm and forearm bones

Clavicle (collarbone)

FRONT OF BODY

22 Skull and facial bones

Carpals (wrist bones)

Hip bone

25 Chest bones

1 Throat bone (behind the chin)

BACK OF BODY

6 Ear bones

4 Shoulder bones

Scapula (shoulder blade)
The broad scapula connects your upper arm to your clavicle.

2 Pelvic bones

26 Vertebrae (bones of the spine)

Humerus (upper arm bone)
This links your shoulder to your lower arm.

Ulna
Your ulna is connected to your radius, your other forearm bone by a flat sheet of ligament

Skeleton facts

Longest bone	Femur (thigh bone)
Smallest bone	Stapes (stirrup bone, in ear)
Strongest bone	Femur (thigh bone)
Densest bone	Temporal bone (in skull)

shape!

Types of bone
You have flat, short, and long bones. You also have a number of irregular bones that are not shaped like any of these three types. The vertebrae of your spine and your facial bones are examples of irregular bones.

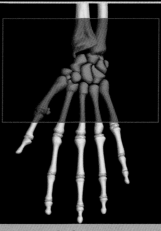
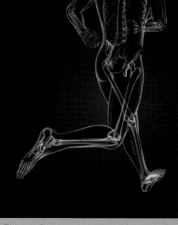

Metacarpals (long hand bones)

Phalanges (finger bones)

Flat bones
Thin, flat bones protect softer tissues. Your flat skull bones, for example, form a "helmet" that keeps your brain safe.

Short, sturdy bones
These block-like bones make small, complex movements. They include the carpals in the wrist and the tarsals in the foot.

Long bones
Large movements involve bones that are longer than they are wide. Your arm and leg bones are long bones.

Phalanges (toe bones)

Metatarsals (long foot bones)

Coccyx (tailbone)
This is the end of your spine. The name means "cuckoo" in Greek.

Patella (kneecap)
Your patella protects your knee joint.

Tibia (shinbone)
This long, robust bone connects your knee to your foot.

Tarsals (ankle bones)

52
Foot bones (total for both feet)

8 Leg bones

Femur (thigh bone)
Your femur has to be incredibly strong to carry your body's weight.

Fibula (calf bone)
The thin fibula supports your ankle.

When will I stop growing taller?
By your mid to late teens, your skeleton is almost fully formed. Girls tend to reach their final heights at about age 16, boys between 18 and 20. But a few bones keep growing. Your clavicle, for example, completes its growth when you are about 25.

Between the ages of 2 and 12, you grow about

6.5 cm (2.5 ins) **every year**

Who's tallest?
Height depends a lot on the lengths of the femurs and tibias in the legs.

54 Hand bones (total for both hands)

ATLAS AXIS

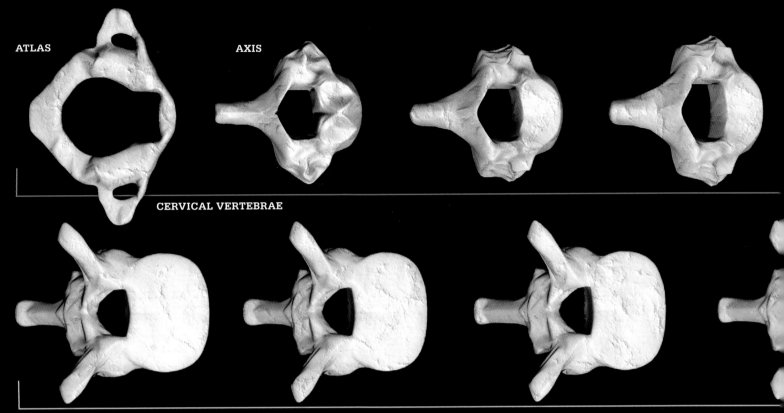

CERVICAL VERTEBRAE

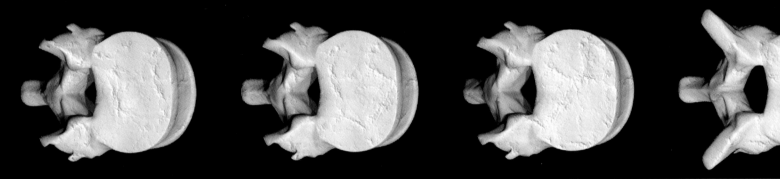

UPPER THORACIC VERTEBRAE

LOWER THORACIC VERTEBRAE

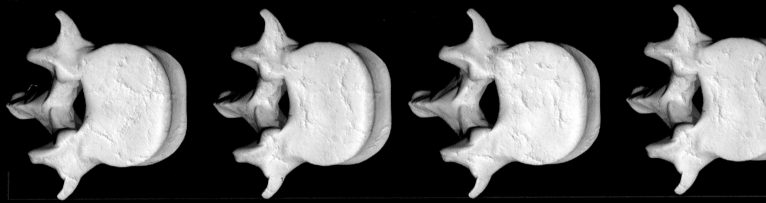

LUMBAR VERTEBRAE

Spine

You have 33 bones in your spine, called
vertebrae. Some of them are fused together,
leaving 26 individual bones. The top vertebrae,
the atlas and the axis, are shaped to allow
your skull to turn and to tilt up and down.

You have

7 vertebr

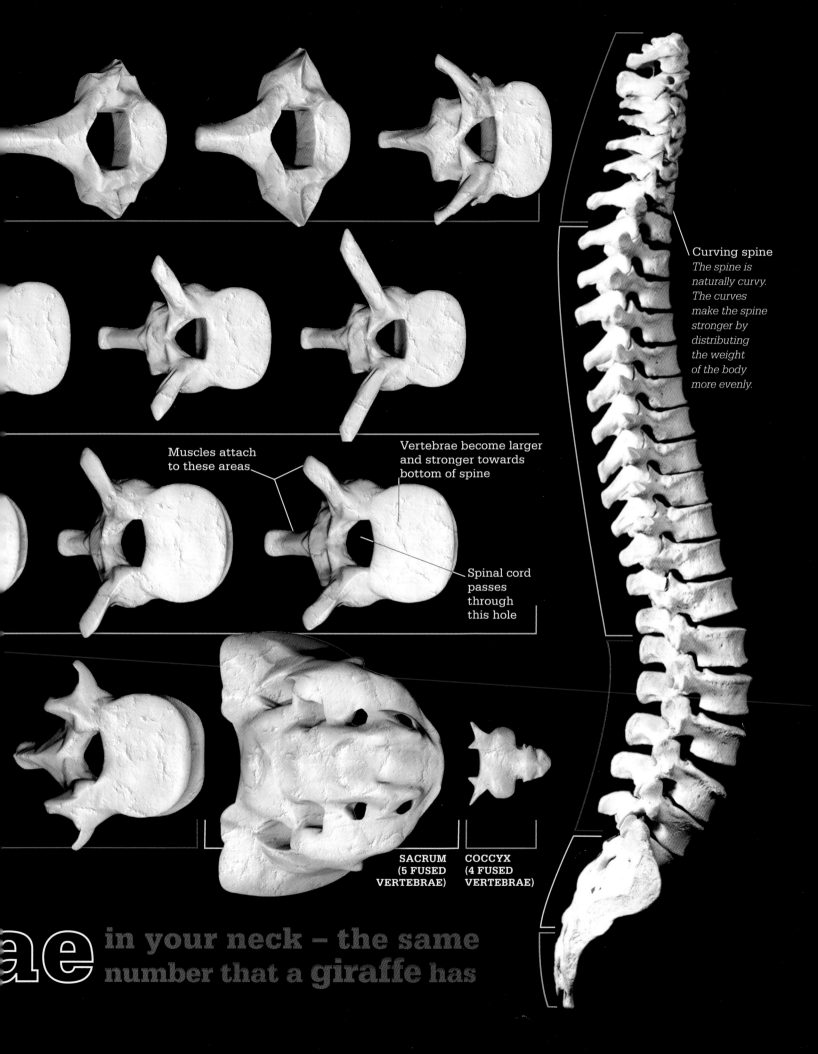

Curving spine
The spine is naturally curvy. The curves make the spine stronger by distributing the weight of the body more evenly.

Muscles attach to these areas

Vertebrae become larger and stronger towards bottom of spine

Spinal cord passes through this hole

SACRUM (5 FUSED VERTEBRAE)

COCCYX (4 FUSED VERTEBRAE)

ae in your neck – the same number that a **giraffe** has

Inside bones [Busy places]

Bones are the body's tough guys. Weight for weight, they are stronger than steel. And bones don't just form your sturdy skeleton. They are living organs, able to grow, repair themselves, and make cells for your blood.

What bones are made of

About 80 percent of your skeleton consists of a hard material called compact bone, and 20 percent is spongy bone. Bone marrow is a flexible tissue found inside bones. Yellow marrow stores fat. Red marrow makes red and white blood cells and platelets.

Cross-section
An individual bone's outside is made of hard compact bone. Inside, an inner core of marrow is ringed by spongy bone.

Periosteum
This is a thin membrane that covers the bone.

Red marrow
All of your red blood cells and 60–70 percent of your white blood cells are made in red bone marrow.

Spongy bone

Bone marrow

Blood vessels

Compact bone

Compact bone
This dense bone has cells called osteocytes, which are surrounded by hard mineral matter. Tiny channels, called canals, carry blood vessels, lymph vessels, and nerves through the bone.

Canal

Osteocyte

Spongy bone
This image of dried spongy bone shows its honeycomb structure, made up of bony struts. The cavities in this type of bone are filled with marrow, making the bone spongy.

Strut

Cavity

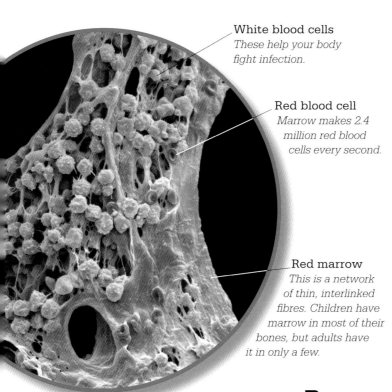

White blood cells
These help your body fight infection.

Red blood cell
Marrow makes 2.4 million red blood cells every second.

Red marrow
This is a network of thin, interlinked fibres. Children have marrow in most of their bones, but adults have it in only a few.

Living bone

Bone is constantly being broken down, then built up again. This process helps maintain bone strength. Cells that break down bone are called osteoclasts. Bone-building cells are called osteoblasts. If a bone breaks, osteoblasts make new bone to repair the break. Osteoclasts help make the new bone the right shape.

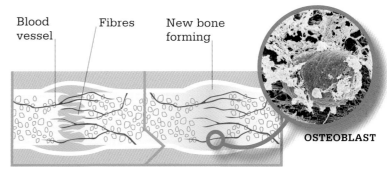

Blood vessel   Fibres   New bone forming

OSTEOBLAST

1 **Bridging the gap**
New blood vessels and tissue fibres grow to link pieces of bone.

2 **Fixing the break**
Osteoblasts deposit minerals in the break to create fresh bone.

Cartilage

The gristly tip of your nose is cartilage – a springy tissue that supports your skeleton. Cartilage comes in three types: hyaline, fibrous, and elastic. Your ears are made mostly of elastic cartilage.

Hyaline cartilage
This covers the ends of bones in joints. It helps them slide smoothly over one another.

RIBS   TIP OF NOSE   JOINTS

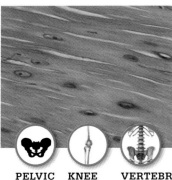

Fibrous cartilage
Like a shock absorber, this cartilage cushions joint bones against jolts and bumps.

PELVIC BONES   KNEE   VERTEBRAE

Bone growth

Osteoblasts were particularly important early in your life. Your skeleton began to develop before you were born. Most of it was cartilage, which served as a template for your future bones. Osteoblasts gradually deposited minerals in the cartilage, changing it into bone.

Bone (purple areas)

Cartilage (white areas)

Hand growth
Here you can see how cartilage in the hand changes to bone.

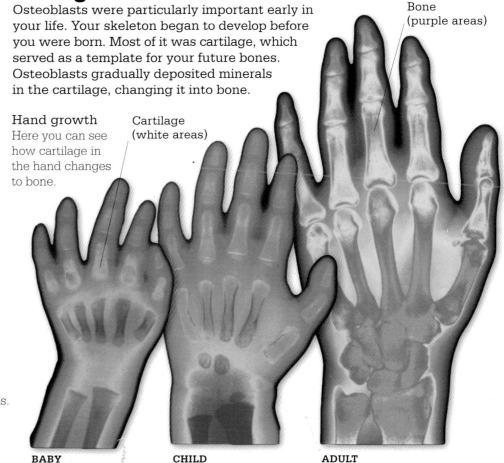

BABY   CHILD   ADULT

Without joints – the places where the ends of bones meet – your body would be rigid like a statue. Most joints can move freely, but a few can move only a little. At birth, your skull bones are linked by tissues that are flexible so that your brain can grow quickly. These joints close up and become fixed by early adulthood.

You have over 200 joints in your body

Slightly movable

Some joints have limited ranges of movement, to make sure that you're stable. The two halves of the pelvis are joined at the front by cartilage (see page 39). This allows just enough movement to absorb shock when you walk or run. The vertebrae in your spine are also separated by shock-absorbing cartilage.

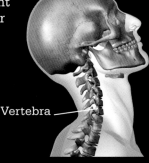

Joints between vertebrae
The slightly movable joints of the spine make it strong and stable, yet flexible, too.

Vertebra

Ligaments

Most joints are made more stable by ligaments. These strips of tough tissue hold bones together and make joints stronger. Ligaments may surround a joint or link bones.

Ligaments

Crossing over
Ligaments in the knee cross each other inside the joint and keep it stable.

Moving joints
Freely moving joints are called synovial joints.

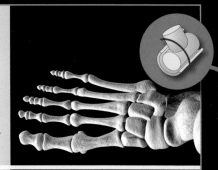

Hinge joint
The joints of your toes and fingers move like door hinges, back and forth. Your knee is also a hinge joint.

Gliding joint
The ends of two flat bones glide over each other so that the bones of the joint can move from side to side.

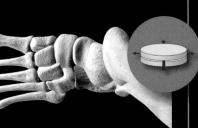

Ball-and-socket joint
The rounded head of one bone fits into the cup-shaped socket of another for a wide range of movements.

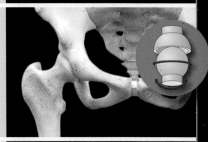

Pivot joint
A peg-like projection on one bone pivots inside the socket of another bone, allowing the joint to rotate.

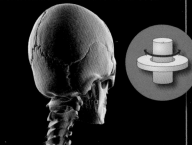

Ellipsoidal joint
The egg-shaped end of one bone fits into the cavity of another and can move side to side and back and forth.

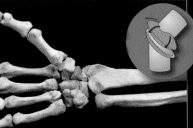

Saddle joint
Two U- or saddle-shaped bone ends fit together at right angles. The joint can rotate in two directions.

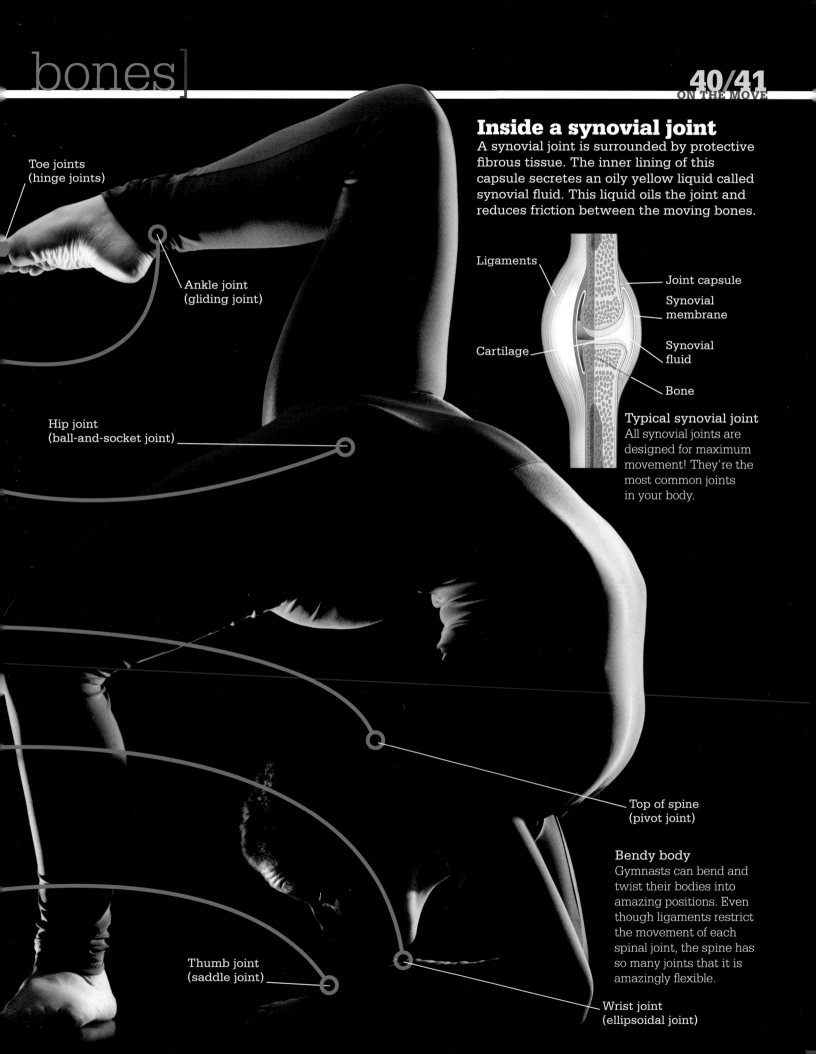

Toe joints
(hinge joints)

Ankle joint
(gliding joint)

Hip joint
(ball-and-socket joint)

Inside a synovial joint

A synovial joint is surrounded by protective fibrous tissue. The inner lining of this capsule secretes an oily yellow liquid called synovial fluid. This liquid oils the joint and reduces friction between the moving bones.

Ligaments

Cartilage

Joint capsule

Synovial membrane

Synovial fluid

Bone

Typical synovial joint

All synovial joints are designed for maximum movement! They're the most common joints in your body.

Top of spine
(pivot joint)

Bendy body

Gymnasts can bend and twist their bodies into amazing positions. Even though ligaments restrict the movement of each spinal joint, the spine has so many joints that it is amazingly flexible.

Thumb joint
(saddle joint)

Wrist joint
(ellipsoidal joint)

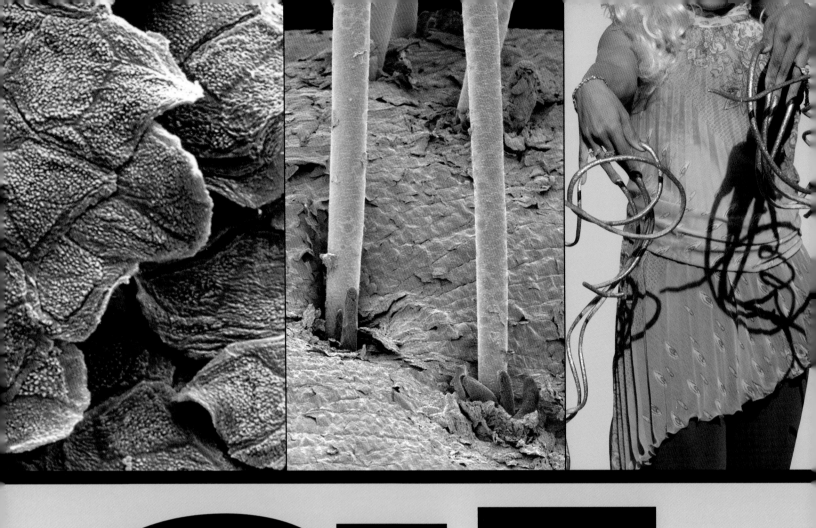

SK

How many skin cells do you lose in a minute?

* Which animal lives in your eyelashes?

Who has the longest nails in the world?

you're in

Through wear and tear, you shed, or lose, about 40,000 skin cells each minute! But don't worry – your skin completely renews itself every 28 days or so. During your whole life, you'll get around 1,000 new "suits" of skin.

Multi-purpose suit

Skin is your best defence against germs. It also filters out harmful ultraviolet (UV) rays from sunlight. It helps keep your body temperature at a stable 37°C (98.6°F). And it makes vitamin D for healthy bones.

Scaly skin
The cells at the very surface of your skin are dead. They are hardened scales of a protein called keratin.

- PROVIDES SUN PROTECTION
- PROVIDES DEFENCE AGAINST INFECTION
- REGULATES BODY TEMPERATURE
- MAKES VITAMIN D

An adult's skin weighs 4 kg (9 lbs)

Big skin
Your skin is your body's largest organ.

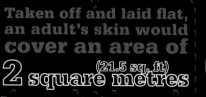
Taken off and laid flat, an adult's skin would **cover an area of 2 square metres** (21.5 sq. ft)

Skin structure

Your skin has two main layers. The waterproof epidermis keeps your body from drying out. The thicker dermis makes your skin flexible and strong.

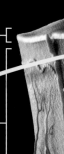

Marvellous melanin
This pigment makes skin dark and produces freckles. It also blocks damaging UV rays.

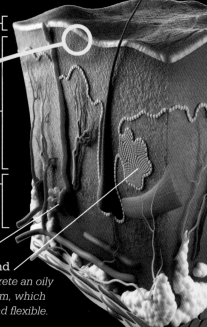

Hair

Epidermis
This thin layer is made up of tough cells.

Dermis
The dermis has blood vessels and nerves.

Fat layer
Fat keeps you warm, and it absorbs shocks.

Sweat gland

Sebaceous gland
These glands secrete an oily liquid called sebum, which keeps skin soft and flexible.

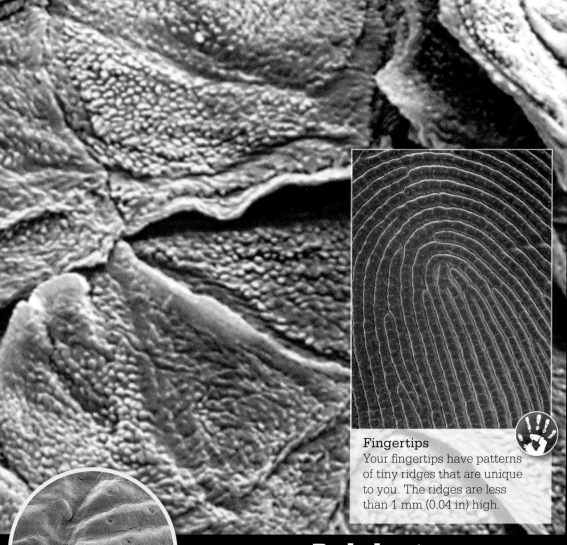

New skin

As old, dead skin cells are shed, fresh cells are pushed up from the base of the epidermis. The closer they get to the surface, the more they fill with keratin.

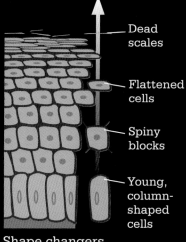

- Dead scales
- Flattened cells
- Spiny blocks
- Young, column-shaped cells

Shape changers

Cells change shape as they move towards the surface, gradually getting flatter.

Fingertips

Your fingertips have patterns of tiny ridges that are unique to you. The ridges are less than 1 mm (0.04 in) high.

Cooler areas (blue/purple)   Warmer areas (red/yellow)

Sweat pores

Sweat oozes out of pores in your skin when you are hot. As it dries, it carries heat away from your body.

Body heat

If you overheat, your skin's blood vessels widen. This lets more blood reach your skin, where it loses heat to the air. If you're too cold, your vessels narrow. This restricts blood flow, reducing heat loss.

Heat loss

These images, taken with a heat-detecting camera, show how the body gives off heat after exercise.

BEFORE EXERCISE   **AFTER EXERCISE**

Skin repair

When you are cut, damaged tissues release alarm chemicals. These kick your body's skin-repair system into action.

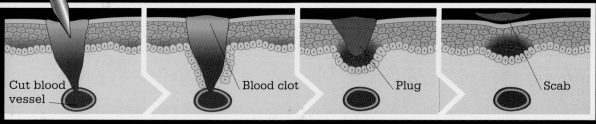

Cut blood vessel   Blood clot   Plug   Scab

1 Sound the alarm
As blood f█████nto the wound, platelets (see page 53) flock to the site.

2 Form a blood clot
Platelets create strands of protein that bind red blood cells into a clot.

3 Plug the wound
The cl██ shrinks and plugs the hole, protecting the wound from infection.

4 Protect with a scab
The clot hardens into a scab, and new skin tissue forms beneath it.

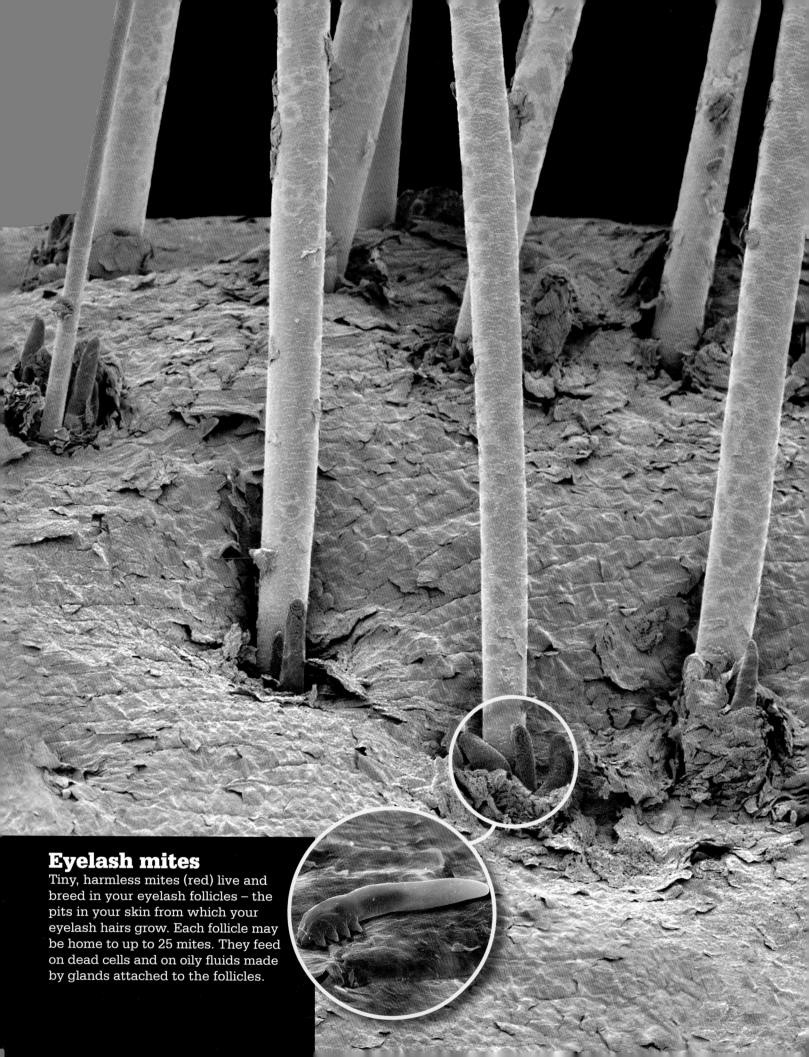

Eyelash mites

Tiny, harmless mites (red) live and breed in your eyelash follicles – the pits in your skin from which your eyelash hairs grow. Each follicle may be home to up to 25 mites. They feed on dead cells and on oily fluids made by glands attached to the follicles.

Head louse

Measuring up to 3 mm (0.1 in) long, head lice sometimes live in human hair. They suck blood through the skin of the scalp and make it itchy. In three weeks, a female louse lays up to 100 eggs, gluing them onto hairs.

Your hair looks fantastic – but it's dead! The only living parts of hair lie under your skin's surface, growing in tiny pits called follicles. The visible hairs you comb and style are made of dead cells.

Hair almost everywhere

Most of the body is covered with short, fine, hard-to-see hairs. Hairless parts of the body include the lips, eyelids, palms of the hands, and soles of the feet.

SCALP HAIR PROTECTS FROM BUMPS, RAIN, AND SUN

EYEBROWS KEEP SWEAT FROM GETTING INTO EYES

NOSTRIL HAIRS KEEP OUT POLLEN AND GERMS

EYELASHES SHIELD EYES FROM DUST

Hair protection
Hairs have different jobs to do, depending on where they grow.

What shape?

Whether your hair is curly or straight depends on the shapes of the follicles out of which the hairs grow. These, in turn, are determined by the genes that you inherited (see pages 101–103).

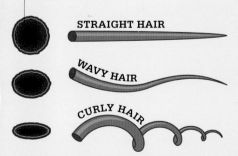

Shape of follicle

STRAIGHT HAIR

WAVY HAIR

CURLY HAIR

Curly, wavy, or straight
A circular follicle produces straight hair. An oval follicle makes wavy or curly hair. The more stretched the oval shape of the follicle, the curlier the hair.

Scalp hairs
The long, coarse hairs on your head grow about 1 cm (0.4 in) each month. The world-record length is 5.5 m (18 ft)!

Strand of hair
Inside each strand are fibres of keratin (see page 44) and the pigment melanin, which gives hair its colour. The outer layer, the cuticle, consists of dead, scaly cells.

Number of scalp follicles in people with
red hair:
80,000
black hair:
108,000
blonde or brown hair:
146,000

Hair

Scalp

Follicle

Facial hair
A boy can usually grow a beard or moustache from the age of about 17.

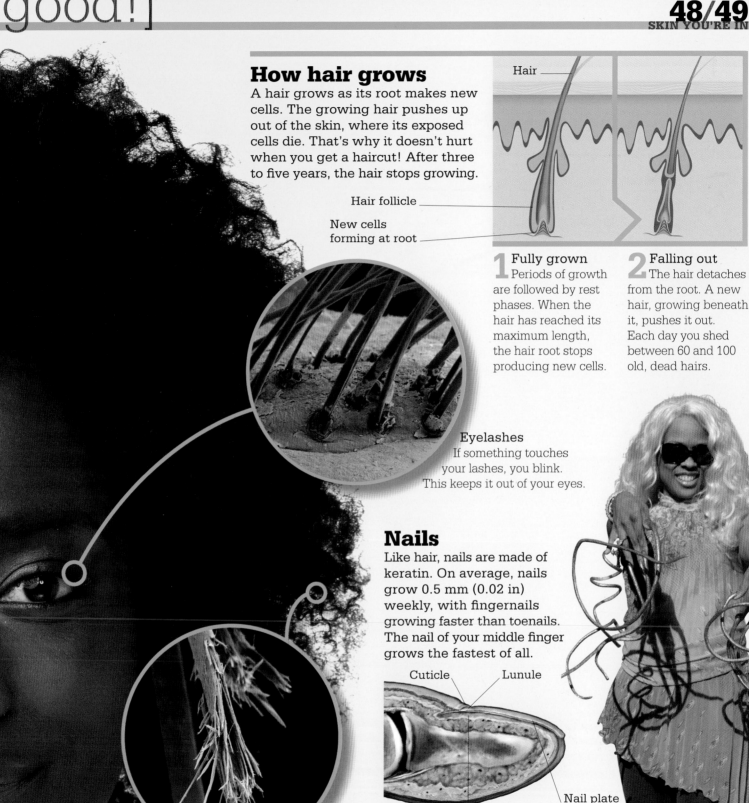

How hair grows

A hair grows as its root makes new cells. The growing hair pushes up out of the skin, where its exposed cells die. That's why it doesn't hurt when you get a haircut! After three to five years, the hair stops growing.

Hair

Hair follicle

New cells forming at root

1 Fully grown
Periods of growth are followed by rest phases. When the hair has reached its maximum length, the hair root stops producing new cells.

2 Falling out
The hair detaches from the root. A new hair, growing beneath it, pushes it out. Each day you shed between 60 and 100 old, dead hairs.

Eyelashes
If something touches your lashes, you blink. This keeps it out of your eyes.

Nails

Like hair, nails are made of keratin. On average, nails grow 0.5 mm (0.02 in) weekly, with fingernails growing faster than toenails. The nail of your middle finger grows the fastest of all.

Cuticle   Lunule

Nail plate

Nail matrix

Split ends
On an old or damaged hair, the cuticle peels off. The keratin fibres below unravel, causing split ends.

Nail anatomy
Cells made by the matrix turn into keratin to form the nail plate. The lunule, a pale semi-circle at the nail's base, is the visible part of the matrix.

World's longest nails
Together, Chris Walton's fingernails measure more than 6 m (20 ft) long!

Body
eng

What sticky stuff can keep a cut from bleeding?

* Where can you find the death zone?

Which insects kill the most people?

ines

Blood on the move

Whizzing around like a miniature race car, a red blood cell takes just 60 seconds to complete one lap of your circulatory system. This vast network of blood vessels extends throughout your entire body.

You have

96,000 (60,000 miles) kilometres of blood vessels

Blood vessels

Arteries carry fresh blood, filled with oxygen and nutrients, from the heart. Veins return used blood containing waste products to the heart after the oxygen and nutrients have been put to work.

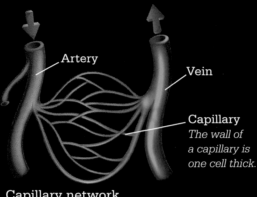

Artery

Vein

Capillary
The wall of a capillary is one cell thick.

Capillary network
Tiny capillaries link arteries and veins. Oxygen and nutrients pass out through their walls, and waste products pass in.

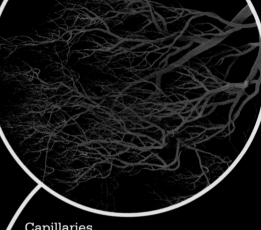

Vein wall
Vein walls are thinner and more flexible.

Capillaries
These vessels are so small that ten would equal the thickness of a human hair.

Artery wall
These walls are strong and muscular.

Inferior vena cava
This is one of two large veins that take used blood to the heart.

Descending aorta
This takes fresh blood to the lower body.

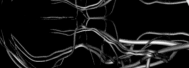

Thin and thick walls
This microscopic view shows a slice through a vein and an artery.

Aorta
This large artery takes fresh blood away from the heart.

Heart

CIRCULATORY SYSTEM

Superior vena cava

What's in blood?

Blood has a liquid part called plasma. Red and white blood cells and platelets float in the plasma. Red blood cells transport oxygen and nutrients; white blood cells defend your body against germs. Platelets are tiny cell fragments that are vital for blood clotting.

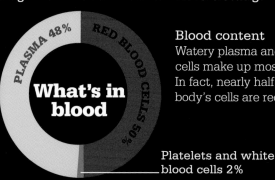

What's in blood

PLASMA 48%

RED BLOOD CELLS 50%

Blood content
Watery plasma and red blood cells make up most of your blood. In fact, nearly half of all your body's cells are red blood cells.

Platelets and white blood cells 2%

Why is my blood red?
Each red blood cell contains about 300 million molecules of haemoglobin, a protein that carries oxygen around the body. Haemoglobin contains iron, which makes blood red. Not all animal blood is red. Horseshoe crabs have blue blood, due to the presence of copper.

Inside an artery
All arteries, except those that take blood to the lungs, carry oxygen-rich blood.

Platelets

These can become sticky and "glue" themselves together to heal a cut (see page 45). They can also trigger the production of the protein fibrin. Fibrin traps red blood cells to form clots and keep blood from leaking out of cuts.

White blood cell

Platelet

Plasma

Red blood cell

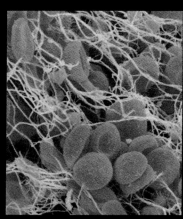

Fibrin net
A net-like mesh of fibrin traps red blood cells to form a clot.

Common iliac artery
The artery takes blood to the pelvis.

Femoral artery
The femoral artery supplies blood to the leg.

There are
5 million
red blood cells in one
drop of blood

Common iliac vein
This vein drains blood from the pelvis.

Femoral vein
Blood from the leg drains into this vein.

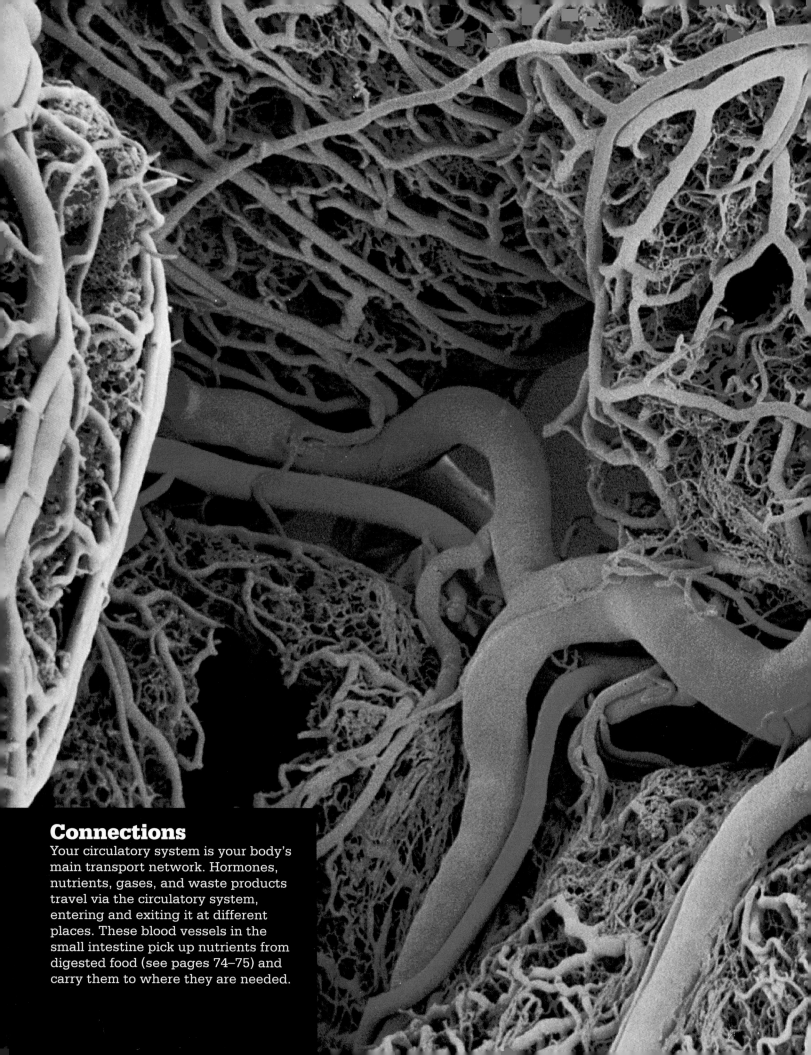

Connections

Your circulatory system is your body's main transport network. Hormones, nutrients, gases, and waste products travel via the circulatory system, entering and exiting it at different places. These blood vessels in the small intestine pick up nutrients from digested food (see pages 74–75) and carry them to where they are needed.

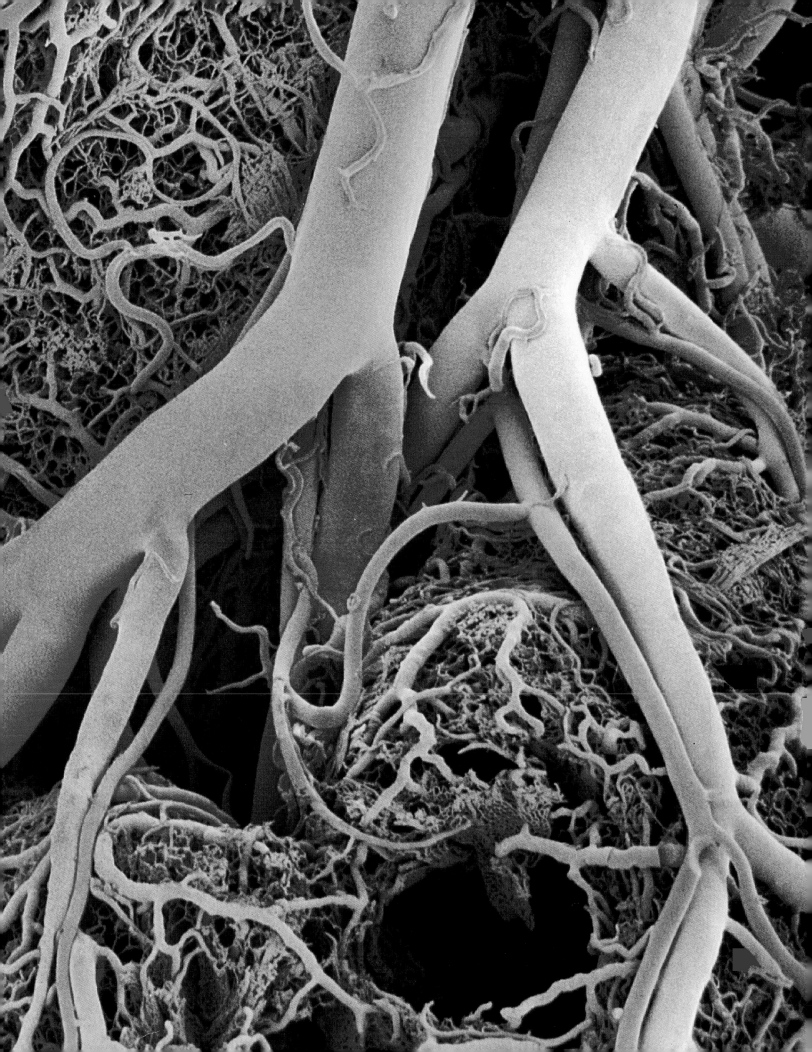

Your heart, made almost entirely of cardiac muscle (see page 31), is the pump that pushes blood around your body. The size of a man's closed fist, it never stops to rest. During a lifetime, it can pump enough blood to fill 90 Olympic swimming pools.

Heart structure

The heart has two upper chambers called atria and two lower chambers called ventricles. It produces electrical signals that tell cardiac muscles to contract. This squeezes the chambers so that they pump blood. The blood travels away from the heart through arteries, and back through veins.

OUTSIDE VIEW OF HEART

Muscle power
Your heart is really just one big muscle that never sleeps! The cells in the muscle work automatically to enable your heart to beat all the time.

Pulmonary artery
This takes blood to the lungs.

Pulmonary vein
This brings blood from the lungs.

Aorta
The aorta takes blood to tissues.

Superior vena cava
This vein brings blood from the upper body.

Septum
This wall of muscle divides the heart into left and right sides.

Right atrium

Cardiac muscle cell

Right ventricle

Inferior vena cava
This vein brings blood from the lower body.

The heart usually beats 60–100x per minute – that's about 100,000 beats per day

Your beating heart
Each heartbeat is a series of rapid actions that allows blood to flow into the heart and then be squeezed out to the lungs or elsewhere.

Right atrium

Left atrium

1 Receiving blood
Used blood from the body enters the right atrium. The left atrium fills with oxygen-rich blood from the lungs.

4 Ventricles contract
Blood is sent from the right ventricle to the lungs and from the left ventricle to the rest of the body.

Blood leaves left ventricle

Blood leaves right ventricle

2 Partial flow
Blood flows from the atria into the ventricles below, until they are about 80 percent full.

Left ventricle

Right ventricle

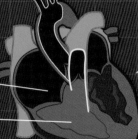

Empty atrium

Full ventricle

3 Atria contract
The atria squeeze the remaining blood into the ventricles. The ventricles are now completely full.

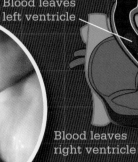

Pulmonary valve
Valves keep blood from flowing the wrong way.

Left atrium

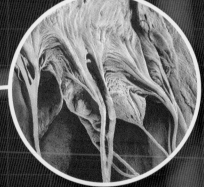

Heart strings
These link the valves to the muscles that open and close them.

Left ventricle

Thick wall
The ventricles have thicker muscular walls than the atria do.

Pericardium
This is a two-layer membrane that protects the heart.

Blood circuits
The pulmonary circuit (green arrows) takes blood to the lungs to pick up oxygen, then brings it back to the heart. The systemic circuit (yellow arrows) takes oxygen-rich blood from the heart to the rest of the body, and returns oxygen-poor blood.

Linked system
The heart links the pulmonary circuit and the systemic circuit to make a single transport system.

UPPER BODY

LUNGS

HEART

LIVER

DIGESTIVE SYSTEM

LOWER BODY

Key
= *Oxygen-poor blood*
= *Oxygen-rich blood*

? What is my pulse?
Each heartbeat sends a wave of high pressure through your arteries. The arteries briefly expand to let the wave pass, then go back to normal. The pulse you can feel on your wrist is the wave passing.

FEELING YOUR PULSE

An elephant heart weighs 20 kg (44 lbs); a human heart weighs less than 0.5 kg (1 lb)

Bad guys

This gallery of villainous germs includes tiny chemical packages, and tapeworms that can grow to up to 10 m (33 ft) in your stomach.

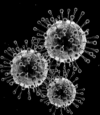

Viruses
A virus invades a living cell and uses it to make copies of itself. There are over 200 cold viruses.

Bacteria
Bacteria are hard to fight, since they multiply rapidly. *E. coli* bacteria cause food poisoning.

Fungi
Fungi can cause mild infections, such as athlete's foot, plus fatal diseases of organs like the lungs.

Protozoa
These are the smallest living animals. A parasite called a Plasmodium is one type of protozoan. It causes malaria.

Tapeworms
Attached to the intestine wall by its mouth, a tapeworm feeds on nutrients in blood.

Body battles [They're

Your body is under siege! Every day, it works hard to keep out disease-causing germs, including bacteria and viruses. Any that break through are hunted down by your body's defence network, the immune system.

Keep out!

Skin is a barrier that keeps germs out. But some sneak in through openings such as the eyes, mouth, and nose. Tears, saliva, and stomach juices contain chemicals that destroy invading germs.

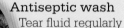

Antiseptic wash
Tear fluid regularly washes over your eyes. It contains chemicals to prevent infection by bacteria.

Sticky tubes
Gooey mucus and tiny hairs line your nose and airways. They trap airborne germs.

Acid barrier
Hydrochloric acid in your stomach kills most of the bacteria that are in the food you eat.

Antibacterial layer
Sebum (see page 44) made by your skin contains substances that attack the cell walls of many bacteria.

Invasion

A wound, or injury, may allow germs into the body. The damaged tissue swells, reddens, and feels hot and painful. This inflammation helps stop the germs from spreading. White blood cells then arrive to attack the invaders.

Ouch!
A tiny cut can let germs into the body. The body reacts rapidly with inflammation.

 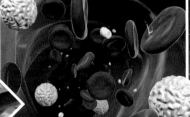 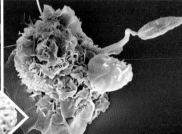

1 Blood flow
When you cut yourself, more blood flows into the injured area. The capillaries widen and their walls become thinner. Fluid leaks out of the blood.

2 To the rescue
Phagocytes and other types of white blood cell arrive at the site. They squeeze through the capillary walls into the fluid between cells.

3 Healing power
The phagocytes surround and digest the invading germs. The blood may also clot (see page 53) to seal the leak and keep more germs from entering.

out to get you!]

Defence network

Your immune system uses white blood cells called lymphocytes to identify and attack specific germs. The lymphocytes remember the intruders if they reappear later.

Doomed cell
Some lymphocytes make proteins called antibodies. These fasten onto germs and infected cells, marking them for destruction.

Lymphatic system
This network of ducts and glands drains lymph, a fluid, from between cells. It also filters out germs and makes and stores lymphocytes.

Thymus
This gland makes lymphocytes.

Spleen
This gland stores lymphocytes and filters germs from the blood.

Lymph node
Nodes (swellings in ducts) filter foreign cells from lymph.

Good guys

Lymphocytes and other types of white blood cell are involved in the fight against infection. White blood cells are made in bone marrow (see page 39). Some are also produced in the lymphatic system.

Cell defenders
There are many types of white blood cell. Some can remember the chemical make-up of a germ, making you immune to it.

T cell receptor
The surface of a T cell is covered with receptors that recognize specific germs.

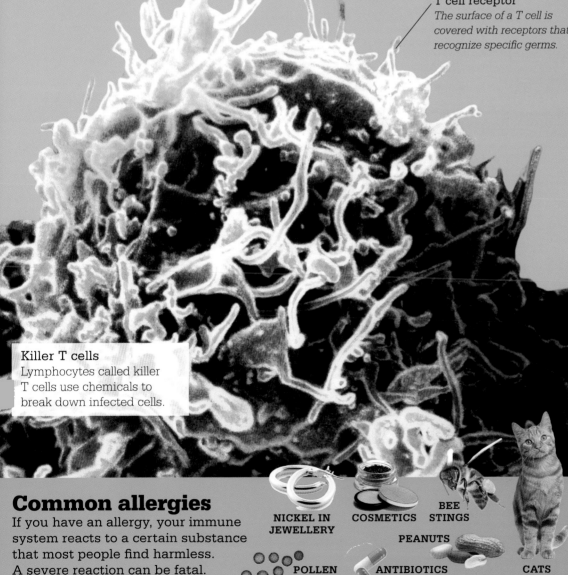

Killer T cells
Lymphocytes called killer T cells use chemicals to break down infected cells.

Common allergies

If you have an allergy, your immune system reacts to a certain substance that most people find harmless. A severe reaction can be fatal.

NICKEL IN JEWELLERY

COSMETICS

BEE STINGS

PEANUTS

POLLEN   ANTIBIOTICS   CATS

Outside help

Sometimes our bodies need a little help to fight infections. Antibiotics are medical drugs that either kill bacteria or keep them from multiplying.

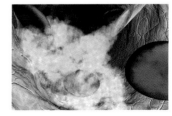

Injection
Antibiotics can be taken as tablets or liquids. They can also be injected directly into the bloodstream.

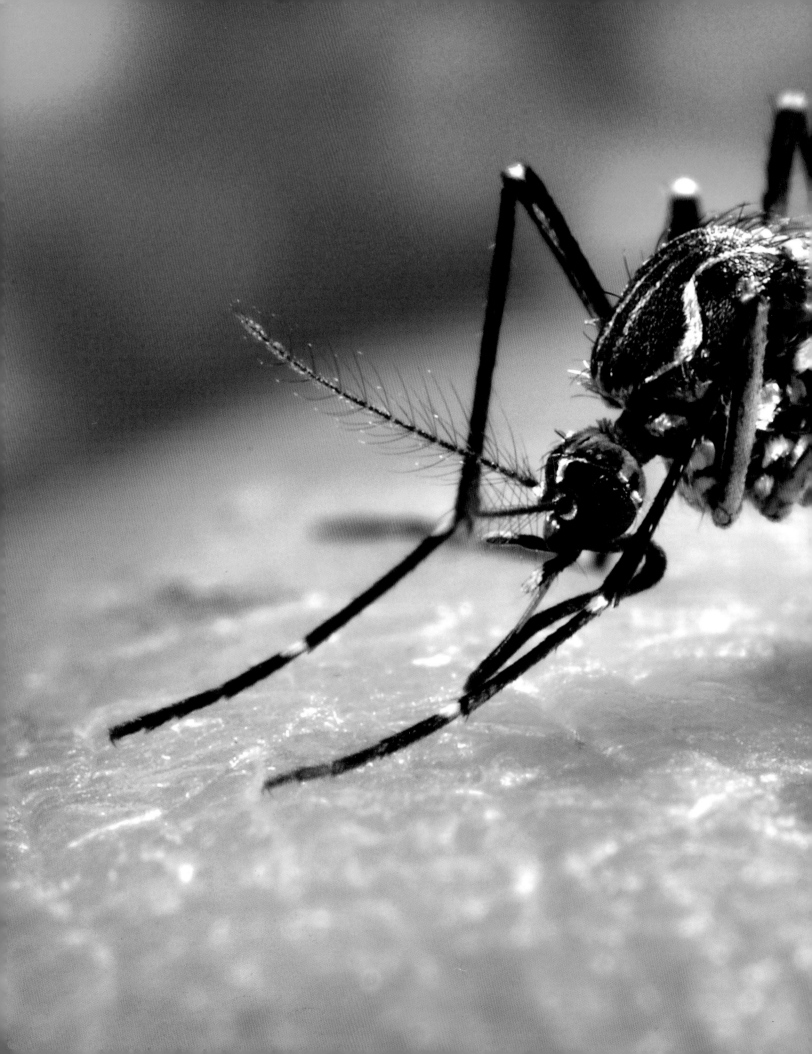

Lethal bite

The body can't always defend itself. As a mosquito feeds on human blood, it can inject parasites from its saliva. This mosquito carries parasites that transmit yellow fever. Around 200,000 people a year contract yellow fever, and 30,000 die. Mosquitoes also carry one of the worst human diseases of all – malaria. Every year, 1 million people die from malaria, especially in Africa and Asia. Victims suffer fevers, headaches, and chills.

Breathing [In and out]

Every day, around 11,000 litres (3,000 gallons) of air pass into and out of the lungs. Air brings in fresh oxygen to fuel body processes and takes away waste carbon dioxide gas. Blood passing through the lungs absorbs the oxygen and then distributes it around the body.

Tube system

When you breathe in air, it passes into the trachea. This tube divides into two smaller tubes called primary bronchi. Each primary bronchus leads to a lung. There, the primary bronchus divides into smaller secondary bronchi, which divide into even smaller tubes called bronchioles.

Safety flap

When you breathe, the epiglottis is open, to let air into the trachea. When you swallow, it shuts, to divert food and liquid into the oesophagus, the tube leading to the stomach.

Nasal cilia
In your nose, tiny hairlike cilia moisten and warm air that is breathed in. They also filter out dust and bacteria.

Oxygen in

Epiglottis

Trachea

Primary bronchus

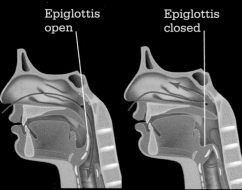

Epiglottis open

Epiglottis closed

BREATHING

SWALLOWING

Keeping food on track
If food goes into your trachea, you choke and cough to bring up the food.

Bronchial cilia
Bronchi are lined with cilia. These move mucus and trapped particles away from the lungs. The mucus is then swallowed or coughed up.

Respiratory system
Your lungs and the tubes leading to them form your respiratory system. The tubes look like an upside-down tree. The smallest "twigs" are the bronchioles. These end in minuscule air sacs (bags) called alveoli.

An average human lung contains over

2,400 km

(1,500 miles) of airways

Right lung

Alveoli
These tiny air bags are surrounded by capillaries. An exchange of gases takes place here (see pages 64–65).

Capillaries

How breathing works

You breathe air in and out by altering the pressure inside your lungs. This is done by contracting and relaxing the rib muscles and a muscular sheet called the diaphragm. This changes the volume (space inside) of the chest cavity.

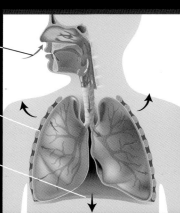
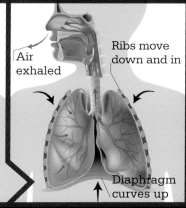

Air inhaled

Ribs move up and out

Diaphragm flattens

Air exhaled

Ribs move down and in

Diaphragm curves up

1 Breathe in (inhale)
The diaphragm and rib muscles contract, increasing the chest's volume, reducing pressure in the lungs, and sucking in air.

2 Breathe out (exhale)
The diaphragm and rib muscles relax, reducing the chest's volume, increasing pressure in the lungs, and expelling air.

Carbon dioxide 0.04%
Other gases 0.06%
Argon 0.9%

Bronchiole

Secondary bronchus

Left lung

Air content

What's in air
Air is a mixture of gases. Your lungs take oxygen from air. They expel the other gases (and some of the oxygen) right away.

? Why can I see my breath when it's cold?

Your mouth and lungs are moist. When you breathe out, water leaves your body along with carbon dioxide. The water is in the form of water vapour, or gas. If it's cold outside, the water vapour cools to its liquid form. You see it as clouds of small droplets in the air.

Gas exchange [The big swap]

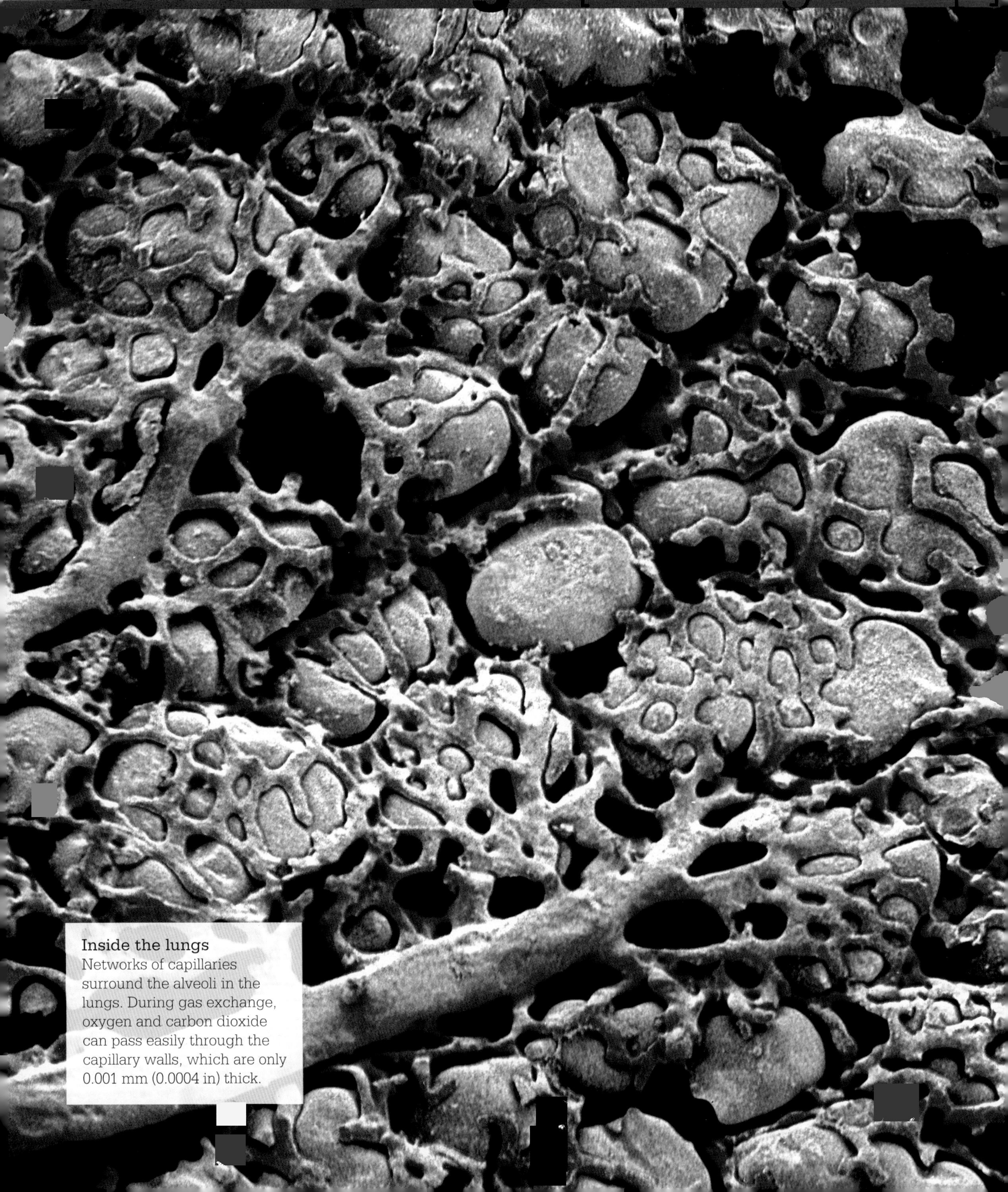

Inside the lungs
Networks of capillaries
surround the alveoli in the
lungs. During gas exchange,
oxygen and carbon dioxide
can pass easily through the
capillary walls, which are only
0.001 mm (0.0004 in) thick.

Packed into your lungs are 300 million alveoli, surrounded by 300,000 capillaries. Together, the alveoli have an enormous surface area of about 70 sq. metres (753 sq. ft), used for gas exchange.

Oxygen supply

Your body cells use oxygen to release the energy they need to survive. This process also releases poisonous carbon dioxide. The two gases pass into and are taken out of your blood in the lungs and body cells.

Capillary   Alveolus

Carbon dioxide enters alveolus

Oxygen enters blood

1 Breathing in
Air enters the lungs and travels to the alveoli. There, oxygen passes through capillaries into the bloodstream and travels to the heart.

4 Breathing out
Blood full of carbon dioxide returns to the heart. From there, it is pumped to the alveoli in the lungs. You get rid of the carbon dioxide by breathing out.

Carbon dioxide enters blood from body cells

3 Exchange of gases
In the cells, the oxygen reacts with glucose to release energy. This produces waste carbon dioxide, which is returned to the bloodstream.

Body cell   Capillary

2 Oxygen to body cells
The heart pumps freshly oxygenated blood around the body. The oxygen passes into body cells through capillaries.

Oxygen enters body cells from blood

On average, an adult at rest uses about
15 litres (4 gallons) of oxygen per hour

Oxygen carrier

Oxygen attaches to molecules of haemoglobin in red blood cells to be transported. Haemoglobin gives blood its red colouring.

OXYGENATED

DEOXYGENATED

Colour of blood
Oxygenated blood is bright red, while deoxygenated blood is darker.

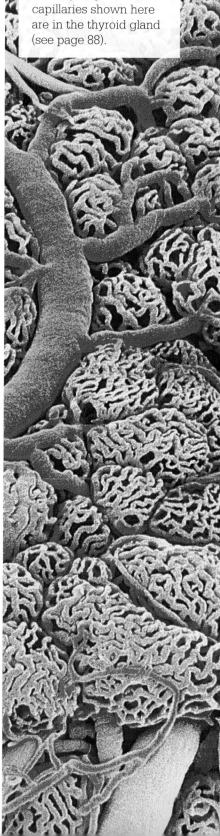

Inside body tissues
Capillaries snake their way through all your body's tissues. They are very fragile. The capillaries shown here are in the thyroid gland (see page 88).

Extreme feats

Venturing to extreme places – such as mountaintops or the deep sea – puts great stress on body tissues and organs. The lungs, especially, find it difficult to cope with unfamiliar conditions.

Out of breath

At high altitudes, air is less dense than it normally is. Each breath of air contains less oxygen than usual. Climbers may need to breathe harder to take in the right amount of oxygen.

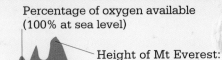

Percentage of oxygen available (100% at sea level)

Height of Mt Everest: 8,848 m (29,029 ft)

5,485 M — **52% O₂** — — — 18,000 FT

1,524 M — **84% O₂** — — — 5,000 FT

SEA LEVEL

Oxygen levels

Altitudes above 8,000 m (26,200 ft) are known as the death zone. People can become very sick, or even die, if their bodies cannot adapt to less oxygen.

Climbing high

Climbers usually carry oxygen supplies to stay healthy on high peaks. But not always. In 1978, Reinhold Messner became the first person to climb Mount Everest, the world's highest peak, without extra oxygen.

pressure]

Into the depths . . .
Christina Sáenz de Santamaría
is an Australian free diver.
During dives, she can hold her
breath for more than 6 minutes.

Deep breath
Most divers use oxygen tanks
underwater. But some daredevil
free divers plunge to great
depths – up to 214 m (700 ft) –
without the help of oxygen tanks.
They simply hold their breath!
The deeper they go, the more
the water pressure increases,
causing their lungs to shrink.

AT SURFACE

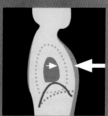

AT DEPTH OF
30 M (100 FT)

Shrinking lungs
At a depth of 30 m (100 ft), water
pressure squeezes the chest in, pushes
the diaphragm up, and shrinks the lungs
to about one-third their normal size.

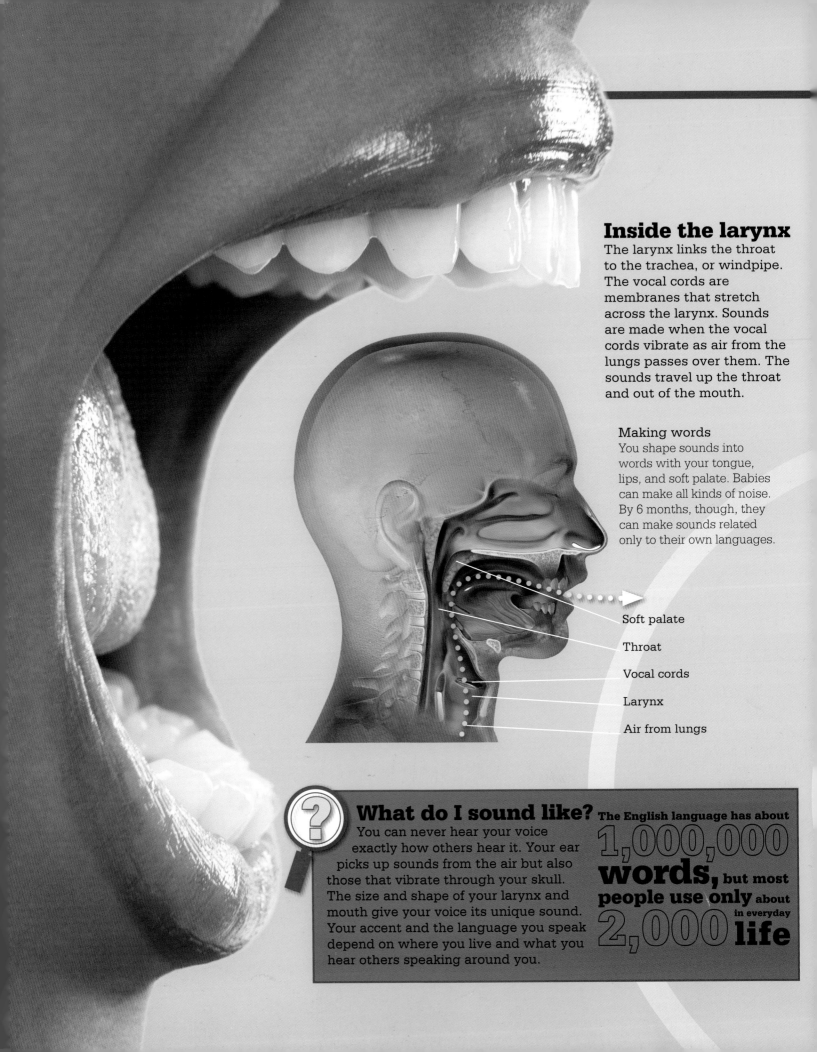

Inside the larynx

The larynx links the throat to the trachea, or windpipe. The vocal cords are membranes that stretch across the larynx. Sounds are made when the vocal cords vibrate as air from the lungs passes over them. The sounds travel up the throat and out of the mouth.

Making words

You shape sounds into words with your tongue, lips, and soft palate. Babies can make all kinds of noise. By 6 months, though, they can make sounds related only to their own languages.

Soft palate

Throat

Vocal cords

Larynx

Air from lungs

What do I sound like?

You can never hear your voice exactly how others hear it. Your ear picks up sounds from the air but also those that vibrate through your skull. The size and shape of your larynx and mouth give your voice its unique sound. Your accent and the language you speak depend on where you live and what you hear others speaking around you.

The English language has about **1,000,000 words,** but most people use only about **2,000** in everyday **life**

Making noise

Open your mouth and sing. Now whisper a secret! Every sound you make is created when air from your lungs passes over your vocal cords. Touch your throat while you speak to feel your vocal cords vibrate.

Explosive cough
A cough clears irritants such as dust and mucus from the airways. The throat and larynx close, raising the air pressure in the lungs. When they open again, air blasts out of the lungs, shaking the vocal cords.

Cough caught on camera
A cough can spray tiny droplets of mucus up to 3 m (10 ft), at speeds of over 160 kph (100 mph).

Keep calm!
Straining your voice will make you hoarse and may damage your vocal cords.

Types of noise
The type, pitch, and volume of the noise you make depend on how tightly stretched your vocal cords are. They also depend on the force of the air from your lungs.

Vocal cords

Cords bang together

Silence
When you are silent, your vocal cords are fully open, so you can breathe.

Speaking
Your vocal cords tighten and pull together. They vibrate as air passes over them.

Whispering
Your vocal cords are slightly stretched and partly open. They do not vibrate.

Screaming
Your cords are shut tight. Air is forced through them, producing a loud, shrill noise.

Having a laugh
Laughing makes you feel good! It's also good for you. It helps you relax and makes your body better at fighting illness. A laugh tends to be a string of the same sound, such as *ho-ho* or *ha-ha*. It's almost impossible to laugh *ho-ha-ho-ha*. Try it!

Children laugh up to 300x a day, but adults laugh an average of only 17x a day!

Fu

Which are the best kinds of food to eat?

* What gases might make you feel embarrassed?

Where can you find 1 million tiny filters?

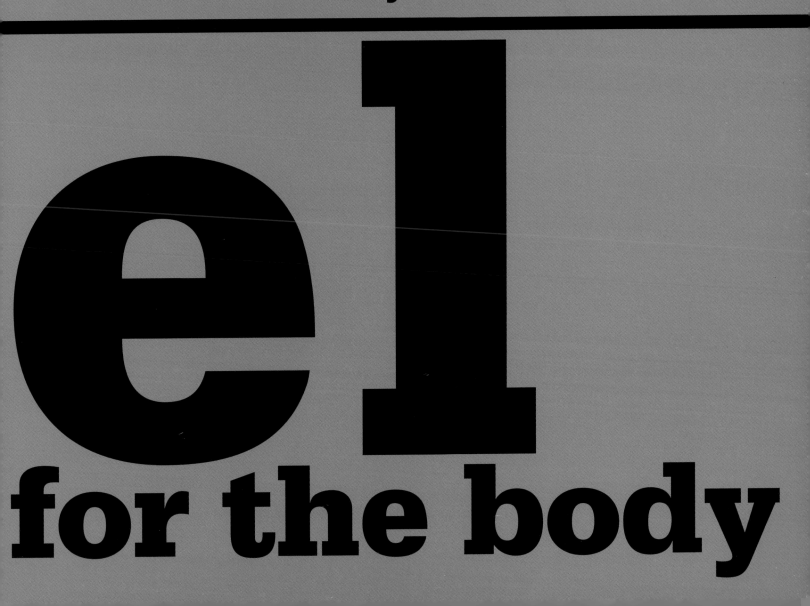

e1
for the body

Eating to live [Yum!]

Fried beetles, barbecued caterpillars, or grilled maggots, anyone? Eating insects may not appeal to you, but they do contain many nutrients – the materials your body needs to stay in tip-top shape. But don't worry! There are other ways to get your nutrients.

Healthy diet

In a healthy diet, about half your food should be vegetables and fruits. You also need plenty of grains, and some proteins. Don't forget to include milk or other dairy products, and make sure you get enough water (see page 24).

In a lifetime, an average person will consume about

27,000 kg (60,000 lbs)

of food

What's in food

Enjoying your food is important! But the main purpose of food is to give your body the nutrients it needs. How much of these types of food do you eat each day?

Proteins

You need protein to build muscle, skin, and bone. It also helps repair injured tissues and can be used to make energy. Meat, beans, fish, and eggs are all protein-rich foods. Surprisingly, chicken is higher in protein than red meat is.

Carbohydrates

Carbohydrates are your main source of energy. Sugar and starch are both carbohydrates. The energy from sugar is short lived. Starch is broken down more slowly, keeping you going for a long time. Starch doesn't have any taste, but it is good for you!

Calorie count

The amount of energy provided by food is measured in calories. You can find out how many calories are in a food by looking at the nutrition label.

Energy use

Calories aren't bad for you – you need them for energy. But if you eat too many or don't burn them off by exercising, your body will store excess calories as fat.

An average-size woman uses 100 calories per hour when standing

An average-size woman uses 600 calories per hour when running

Approximately 70 percent of your brain is fat!

Vitamins and minerals

You need about 30 of these every day – but only in tiny amounts! Your body needs them to work properly. They help you grow and develop.

Name	Needed for	Source
Vitamins		
Vitamin A	Growth, healthy eyes and bones, fighting germs	Salmon
Vitamin B	Making proteins and enzymes, making energy	Cereal
Vitamin C	Good vision, bone and tissue growth, fighting germs	Oranges
Vitamin D	Healthy bones, getting calcium from food	Eggs
Vitamin E	Healthy enzymes, making red blood cells	Nuts
Minerals		
Zinc	Healing the body, making enzymes and proteins	Bread
Calcium	Bones and teeth, healthy nerves, blood clotting	Cheese
Iron	Haemoglobin (carries oxygen in red blood cells)	Spinach
Magnesium	Healthy nerves and muscles, building bones	Green veg
Potassium	Heart, muscle, and cell function, healthy nerves	Bananas
Chlorine	Acid in stomach, keeping body fluids in balance	Salt

Fats

Fats give you energy. They also help your body take in nutrients and build cells. Liquid fats are called oils. The oils in olives, nuts, seeds, and some fish are good for your brain and heart. But don't eat too much solid fat, such as butter!

Fibre

You need fibre to help move food through your digestive system. Lots of brown foods, such as whole wheat bread, are high in fibre, and so are many colourful fruits.

Foods to limit

Fizzy drinks, sweets, and biscuits are full of sugar. They contain lots of calories but few nutrients. They are also bad for your teeth and can cause tooth decay.

Sugar rush

Foods full of sugar give you quick energy, but the effects don't last.

Food's journey

When you eat, food begins a journey through a 9-m (30-ft) long tube called the digestive tract. On the way, your digestive system processes the food and filters out all the bits you need.

The small intestine measures about
7 m (23 ft) –
about the same as a reticulated python, the world's longest snake!

Digestive system
Your body needs food to give it energy, vitamins, and minerals. The food must be broken down, in stages, into substances that your organs and cells can use. This is the job of your digestive system.

Salivary gland
When you taste or smell food, you produce lots of saliva. Saliva moistens food, to make it easy to chew, and contains enzymes that start to break some food down.

Stomach
Tiny glands in the stomach wall make gastric juice. This watery fluid consists of hydrochloric acid and digestive enzymes, which break down food.

Oesophagus
This tube extends from the throat to the stomach.

Tongue

Mouth

Teeth

Pharynx (throat)

Dentine

Enamel

Pulp

Blood vessels and nerves

Gum

Bone

Gall bladder

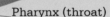

Tough teeth
A tooth has a coating of enamel, the hardest substance in the body. Under this is a bone-like tissue called dentine, and a core of soft pulp.

Clock-watching
Some foods leave the body in less than 12 hours, but usually the time from dinner table to toilet is 24 to 72 hours. Fatty and starchy foods digest slowly. Fruits and fish digest fast.

30–60 SECONDS CHEWING	1–3 SECONDS SWALLOWING	5–8 SECONDS TO STOMACH

1 Chewing
The teeth and tongue mash up food, mix it with saliva, and form it into a ball called a bolus. Enzymes in the saliva start to digest starch in the food.

2 Swallowing
The tongue moves the bolus to the back of the mouth. Muscle contractions in the pharynx (throat) push the bolus towards the oesophagus.

3 To the stomach
Waves of contractions pass through the layers of muscle in the oesophagus wall. They move the bolus of food down towards the stomach.

to bottom]

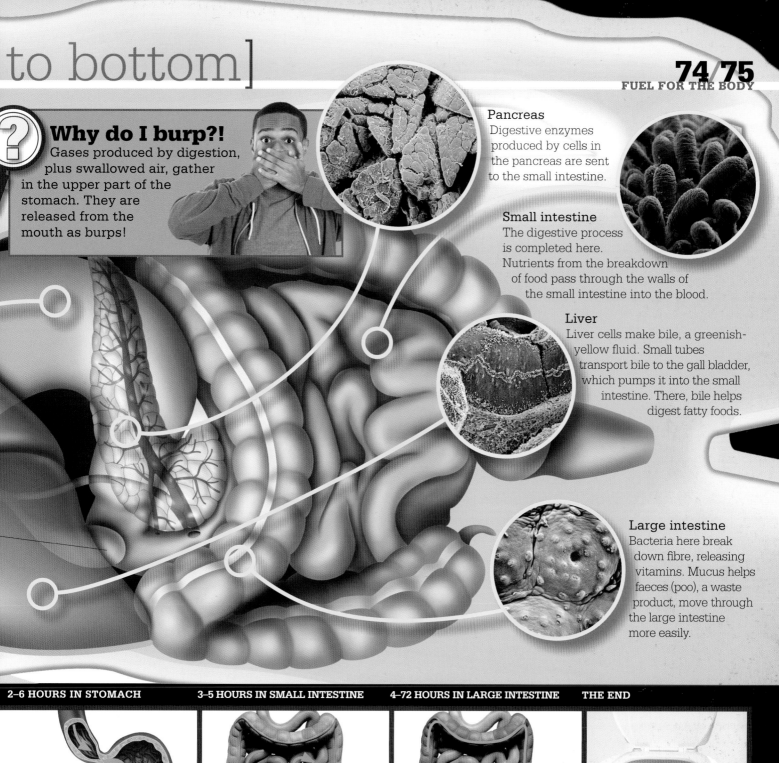

Why do I burp?!
Gases produced by digestion, plus swallowed air, gather in the upper part of the stomach. They are released from the mouth as burps!

Pancreas
Digestive enzymes produced by cells in the pancreas are sent to the small intestine.

Small intestine
The digestive process is completed here. Nutrients from the breakdown of food pass through the walls of the small intestine into the blood.

Liver
Liver cells make bile, a greenish-yellow fluid. Small tubes transport bile to the gall bladder, which pumps it into the small intestine. There, bile helps digest fatty foods.

Large intestine
Bacteria here break down fibre, releasing vitamins. Mucus helps faeces (poo), a waste product, move through the large intestine more easily.

| 2–6 HOURS IN STOMACH | 3–5 HOURS IN SMALL INTESTINE | 4–72 HOURS IN LARGE INTESTINE | THE END |

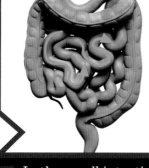
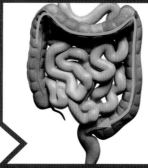
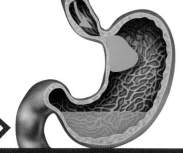

4 In the stomach
The food is mixed with gastric juices to break it down. Muscles contract to reduce the food to a thick, milky material called chyme.

5 In the small intestine
More enzymes are added to the chyme to complete digestion. Nutrients and water pass through the walls into the blood. Waste is left behind.

6 In the large intestine
The waste moves into the large intestine. About 90 percent of the remaining water is removed, leaving semi-solid waste called faeces.

7 The end of the journey
Faeces are held in the rectum. They leave the body via an opening called the anus, which is controlled by muscles called sphincters.

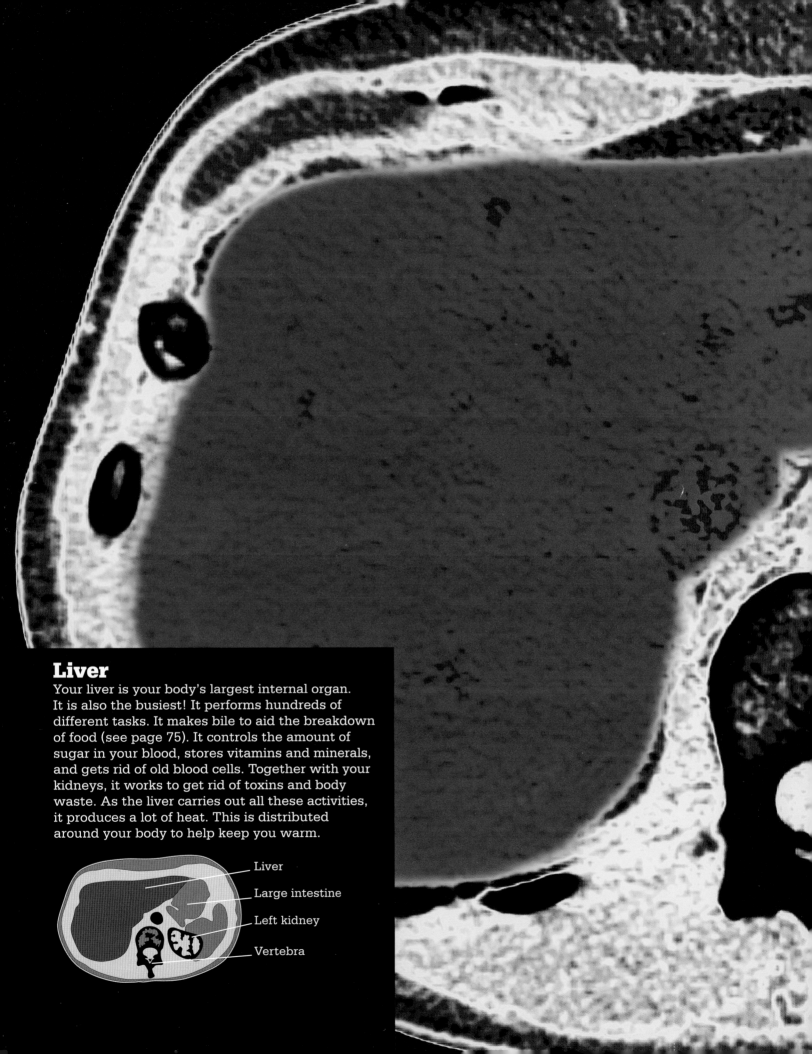

Liver

Your liver is your body's largest internal organ. It is also the busiest! It performs hundreds of different tasks. It makes bile to aid the breakdown of food (see page 75). It controls the amount of sugar in your blood, stores vitamins and minerals, and gets rid of old blood cells. Together with your kidneys, it works to get rid of toxins and body waste. As the liver carries out all these activities, it produces a lot of heat. This is distributed around your body to help keep you warm.

Liver

Large intestine

Left kidney

Vertebra

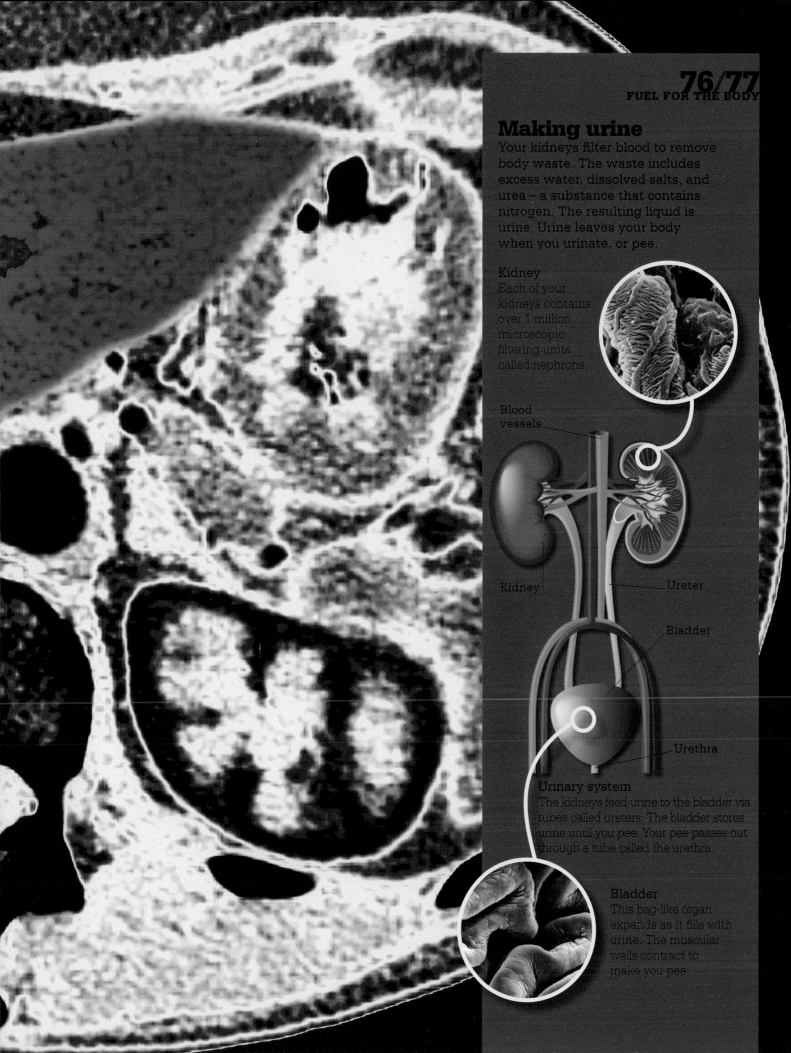

Making urine

Your kidneys filter blood to remove body waste. The waste includes excess water, dissolved salts, and urea – a substance that contains nitrogen. The resulting liquid is urine. Urine leaves your body when you urinate, or pee.

Kidney
Each of your kidneys contains over 1 million microscopic filtering units called nephrons.

Blood vessels

Kidney

Ureter

Bladder

Urethra

Urinary system
The kidneys feed urine to the bladder via tubes called ureters. The bladder stores urine until you pee. Your pee passes out through a tube called the urethra.

Bladder
This bag-like organ expands as it fills with urine. The muscular walls contract to make you pee.

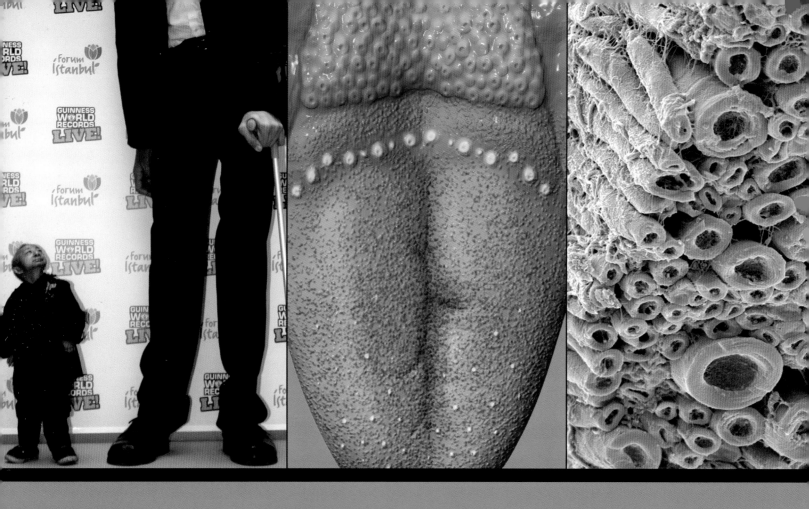

In
con

- What tiny gland might make you grow very tall?

* How do the bumps on your tongue help you taste?

- Which cells with long fibres send electrical messages?

trol

Nerves [Wired up]

If you want to scratch your nose, your brain has to send a signal to your finger! It does this by using part of the vast network of nerves in your body. Nerve cells, or neurons, carry the signal.

There are about 85 billion neurons in the human brain

Nervous system

The brain and spinal cord form the central nervous system (CNS). Peripheral nerves branch out to reach the rest of the body. Neurons carry signals from the CNS to tell the body what to do. They also carry signals from the body back to the CNS.

Spinal cord
The spinal cord is a long, thin tube that runs from the base of your brain down your back. It connects your brain to the rest of your body and is protected by bony vertebrae (see pages 36–37).

Cross-section of spinal cord

Ulnar nerve
This nerve is directly connected to your little finger and other parts of your hand.

Facial nerve
This controls the release of saliva and tears, and relays signals from your tongue.

Brain

Cranial nerves
Many of these connect the sense organs to the brain.

Radial nerve
This large nerve runs down your arm to your wrist and the back of your hand.

? Why do I blink?
Blinking protects your eyes from particles such as dust. The message that there is dust does not travel to the brain so that it can make a decision about whether to blink. Instead, the spinal cord sends a signal via the nerves to make you blink. This is called a reflex action.

On average, you blink 6–20 times every minute

Quick reflex
Reflex actions happen automatically and very quickly.

Inside nerves

Nerves are made up of bundles of neurons, which carry electrical signals. Sensory neurons send messages from your senses to the CNS. Motor neurons send signals away from the CNS to other parts of your body. Interneurons connect sensory and motor neurons.

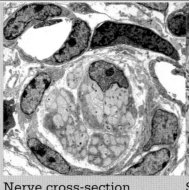

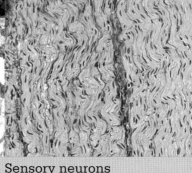

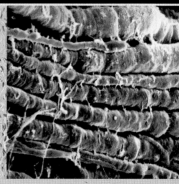

Nerve cross-section
Inside a nerve are nerve bundles (yellow), which contain neurons. Strong tissues surround nerves to protect them from damage.

Sensory neurons
These carry signals from sense organs such as the eyes. They also tell the CNS about internal activities such as heart rate.

Motor neurons
These neurons transmit signals from the CNS to muscles and glands, which then carry out actions.

Femoral nerve
This works the muscles of your thigh, allowing your knee to bend.

Common peroneal nerve
This branch of the sciatic nerve works the muscles of your leg that bend your foot and toes upwards.

Deep peroneal nerve

Lateral plantar nerve
This is the smaller of two branches from the tibial nerve. It links to muscles in the sole and toes.

Saphenous nerve

Tibial nerve
This branch of the sciatic nerve works the muscles of your leg that bend your foot and toes downwards.

Medial plantar nerve
This is the larger of two branches from the tibial nerve. It links to muscles in the sole and toes.

Sciatic nerve
Up to 2 cm (0.8 in) across, this is the thickest nerve in your body. It is also the longest, travelling from your lower spine all the way down to your foot.

Neurons at work

Nerve cells, or neurons, are the oldest and longest cells in your body. They constantly fire messages to one another in the form of electrical signals. Very active neurons fire 100–200 times per second. A few can send up to 1,000 signals per second. They are not replaced when they die.

Nearby neuron

Cell body
The cell body (see page 26) contains all the structures needed to keep the neuron alive.

Synapse
At a synapse, the end of an axon links with another neuron. The two are separated by a tiny gap and do not touch.

Wiring the body

A neuron consists of a cell body, an axon, and several dendrites. Neurons link together like the intricate wiring of a computer's circuitry. They meet one another at special junctions called synapses.

Dendrite
Tentacle-like projections called dendrites carry nerve signals from other neurons to the cell body.

The fastest nerve signals travel at
400 kph, (250 mph)
faster than a Formula 1 car!

[Connections]

Myelin sheath
Resembling a string of sausages around the axon, this helps the nerve signals travel quickly and efficiently. If it is damaged, the signals slow down.

Axon
Also called a nerve fibre, the axon carries nerve signals away from the cell body to other neurons.

Axon

Schwann cell
Each Schwann cell may coil around the axon up to 100 times.

Axon cross section
A series of Schwann cells surrounds the axon to form the myelin sheath. Myelin insulates the axon, keeping the electrical signals inside strong.

Node of Ranvier
This tiny gap between the myelin segments allows nutrients and waste to enter and exit the neuron.

Schwann cell nucleus

Passing on the message
Chemicals called neurotransmitters carry signals from one neuron to another across the gaps at synapses.

Sac of neurotransmitters

1 Chemical release
Neurotransmitters are released when a signal reaches the end of the axon.

End of axon

Synapse

3 Signal triggered
The neurotransmitters trigger an identical signal in the receiving neuron, continuing the signal's journey.

Astrocyte
Star-shaped astrocytes nourish, physically support, and repair neurons.

2 Chemicals received
The neurotransmitters travel across the synapse and slot into receptors on the receiving neuron.

Receiving neuron

That's some nerve!

No, it's not a close-up of an octopus' tentacle – it's a slice through a nerve bundle (see page 81). Each axon (shown in blue) is surrounded by a myelin sheath (yellow). Tough tissue (pink) surrounds the nerve bundle.

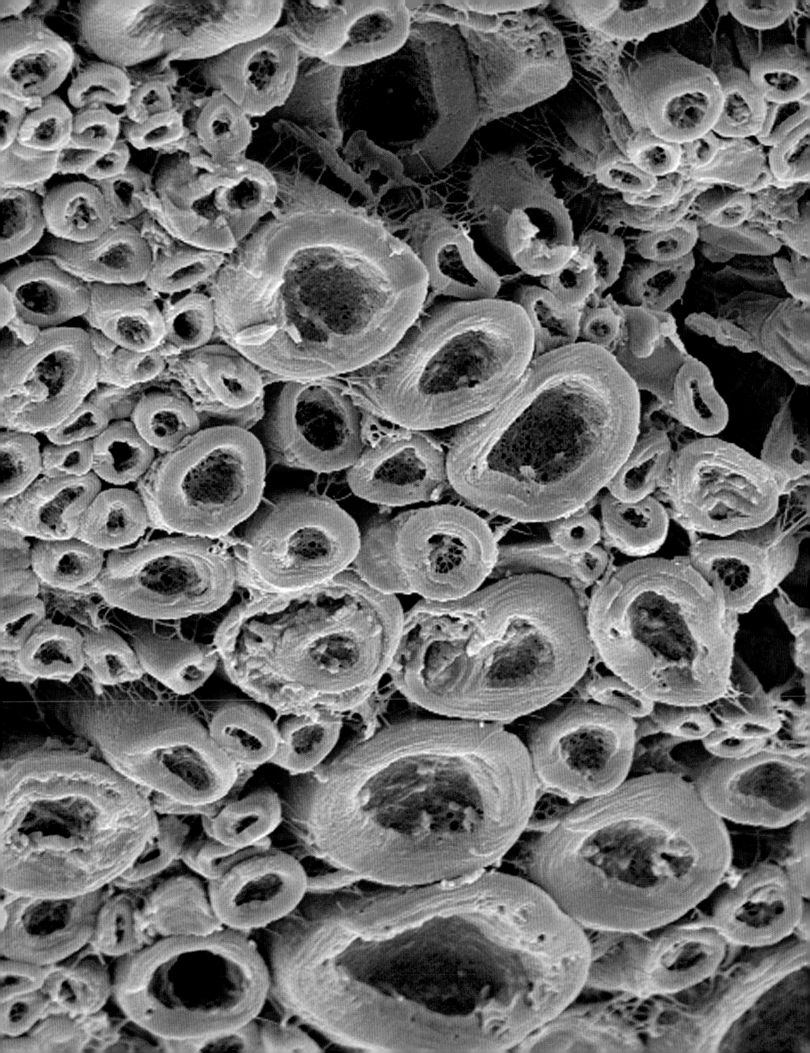

Brain [Control centre]

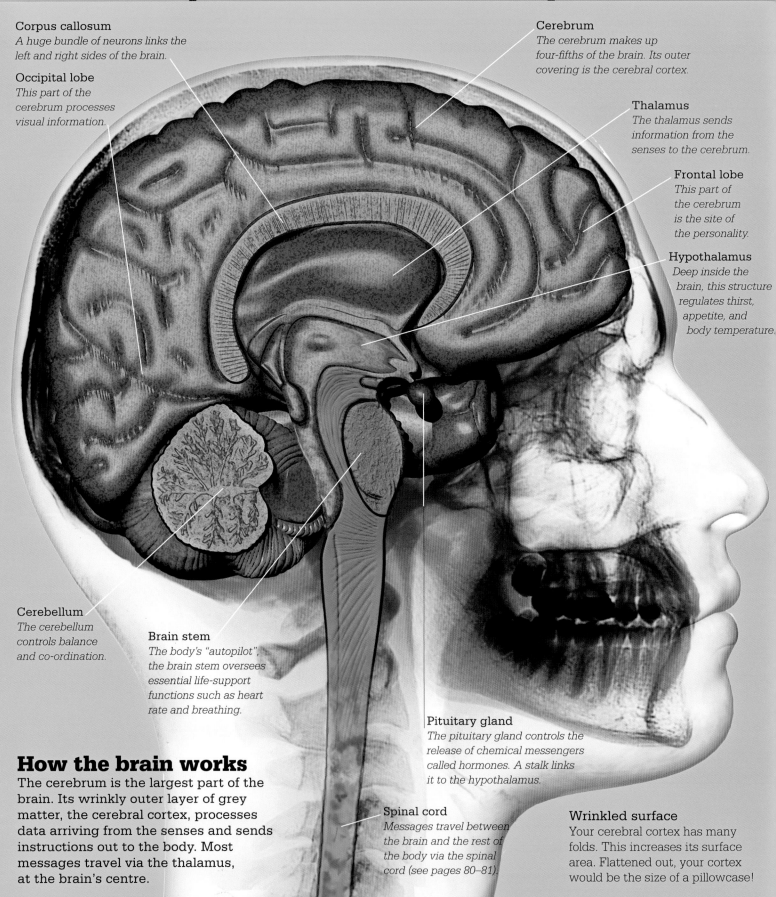

Corpus callosum
A huge bundle of neurons links the left and right sides of the brain.

Occipital lobe
This part of the cerebrum processes visual information.

Cerebrum
The cerebrum makes up four-fifths of the brain. Its outer covering is the cerebral cortex.

Thalamus
The thalamus sends information from the senses to the cerebrum.

Frontal lobe
This part of the cerebrum is the site of the personality.

Hypothalamus
Deep inside the brain, this structure regulates thirst, appetite, and body temperature.

Cerebellum
The cerebellum controls balance and co-ordination.

Brain stem
The body's "autopilot", the brain stem oversees essential life-support functions such as heart rate and breathing.

Pituitary gland
The pituitary gland controls the release of chemical messengers called hormones. A stalk links it to the hypothalamus.

Spinal cord
Messages travel between the brain and the rest of the body via the spinal cord (see pages 80–81).

How the brain works
The cerebrum is the largest part of the brain. Its wrinkly outer layer of grey matter, the cerebral cortex, processes data arriving from the senses and sends instructions out to the body. Most messages travel via the thalamus, at the brain's centre.

Wrinkled surface
Your cerebral cortex has many folds. This increases its surface area. Flattened out, your cortex would be the size of a pillowcase!

A grey lump with the consistency of a soft-boiled egg – your brain doesn't seem impressive. But it controls your body and everything that makes you the person you are: your thoughts, memories, and emotions. It is packed with billions of neurons that process and respond to sensations and experiences, and enable your brain to store vast amounts of data.

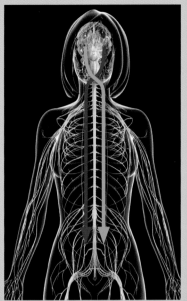

Two halves

The cerebrum is divided down the middle into two halves, called hemispheres. Each has its own speciality. The left half handles language, number skills, and problem-solving. The right half deals with practical and artistic tasks, such as painting.

Crossover
The brain's left half controls the right side of the body, while its right half controls the left side.

Limbic system

Deep in the brain is a group of structures that form the limbic system. This is your body's emotion factory. It controls your feelings and mood swings.

Processing centre
Sensations and experiences arrive at the limbic system. They are sorted and sent to storage as memories in different parts of the brain.

Brain matter

The brain has grey and white matter. Grey matter handles complex tasks and deliberate actions. White matter enables communication between areas of grey matter and the rest of the body.

Where it is
Grey matter is the outer cerebral cortex; white matter is underneath and fills nearly half your cerebrum.

Right half of cerebrum

White matter

Grey matter (cerebral cortex)

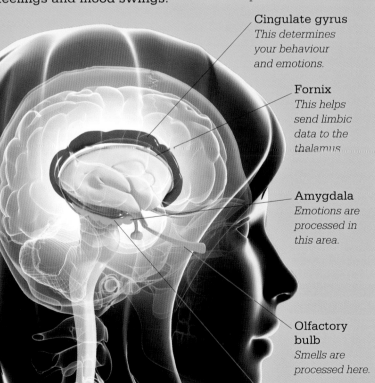

Cingulate gyrus
This determines your behaviour and emotions.

Fornix
This helps send limbic data to the thalamus.

Amygdala
Emotions are processed in this area.

Olfactory bulb
Smells are processed here.

Hippocampus
This area is involved in learning and memory.

Brainpower!

Humans have more brain neurons with more connections between them than any other species does. This means that we can cope with tasks more complex than any other animal can handle.

CHIMPANZEE BRAIN = 6,000,000,000 NEURONS

HUMAN BRAIN = 85,000,000,000 NEURONS

HONEYBEE BRAIN = 950,000 NEURONS

OCTOPUS BRAIN = 300,000,000 NEURONS

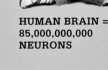

Hormones [Chemical signals]

Hormones put you to sleep. They can also save your life by firing up your body in an emergency. Hormones travel in your blood, even when you're asleep. They take messages to all parts of your body, controlling and co-ordinating bodily functions.

What gland where?

Your body makes over 50 hormones. They are made inside organs called glands and in some tissues. All your hormone-producing tissues and glands together are called the endocrine system.

Hypothalamus
This lies deep inside your brain. It controls the activity of the pituitary gland.

Hypothalamus

Pineal gland
This releases the hormone melatonin, which controls your waking and sleeping patterns.

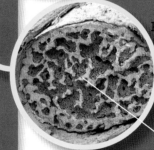

Pituitary gland
This master gland produces hormones that control many functions of other glands. It is the size of a pea.

Pituitary gland

Thyroid gland
The hormone thyroxine, made by this gland, controls how much energy your cells use and regulates your body temperature.

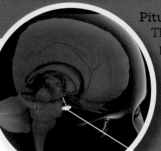

Parathyroid glands
These control the level of calcium in blood and bones.

Bone containing calcium

Thymus gland
Hormones from the thymus help cells called T cells identify germs in blood.

T cell

Pancreas
Your pancreas releases the hormones insulin and glucagon. These help regulate the level of sugar in your blood.

Adrenal glands
Two adrenal glands, one on top of each kidney, produce several hormones. One of these, adrenaline, prepares your body for stress or danger.

I'm so excited!
Your body releases adrenaline if you're excited, angry, afraid, or stressed.

When hormones go wrong

When hormones are not produced in the right quantities, they can cause problems. Growth hormone is produced by the pituitary gland.

Tallest of the tall

The world's tallest man, Sultan Kösen, is 2.5 m (8 ft 3 ins) tall. He is shown here in 2010, standing beside He Pingping, who was just 0.75 m (2 ft 5 ins). Kösen's body produced too much growth hormone during his youth.

Got to run!

When you are afraid, your body's "fight-or-flight" response kicks in. Controlled by the hypothalamus, it uses hormones to get your body ready to defend itself, or to escape.

Message to brain

Hypothalamus

Pituitary gland

Blood vessels
More blood is diverted to the major muscles.

1 Eeek – a spider!
Your brain sends a "distress call" to the hypothalamus, which fires off nerve signals and uses hormones to activate the pituitary gland.

Nerve signals

Adrenal gland

Kidney

HEART   MUSCLES

4 Ready . . .
Adrenaline makes you breathe faster (to take in more oxygen), makes your heart beat faster, and tells your liver to release glucose into your blood. This sends extra oxygen and glucose to your brain and muscles to fuel sudden action.

Muscles
Your skeletal muscles tense up, so you're ready to run.

2 Action stations!
Nerve signals prepare your heart and skeletal muscles for action. You also start to sweat, to keep you cool if you need to run away, and digestion stops.

3 Adrenal rush
The pituitary secretes a hormone that tells the adrenal glands to release adrenaline. You become more alert and experience things more intensely.

5 Run away!
. . . if you're scared of spiders!

Touch [Under the skin]

Your whole body is sensitive to touch, thanks to tiny receptors in your skin. But some parts are more sensitive than others are. Your fingertips, for example, are 100 times more sensitive than your back is. Receptors link to nerves that send signals about what you're touching to your brain.

Receptors

Some receptors respond to forces such as pressure. Others respond to pain, heat, or cold. Receptors consist of the ends of nerve fibres. These may be enclosed in capsules; if not, they are called free nerve endings.

Where it happens

Touch receptors are found mainly in the dermis – the lower of the two layers of skin (see page 44). Receptors for light touch lie near the top of the dermis, while those that detect strong pressure are deeper, close to its base.

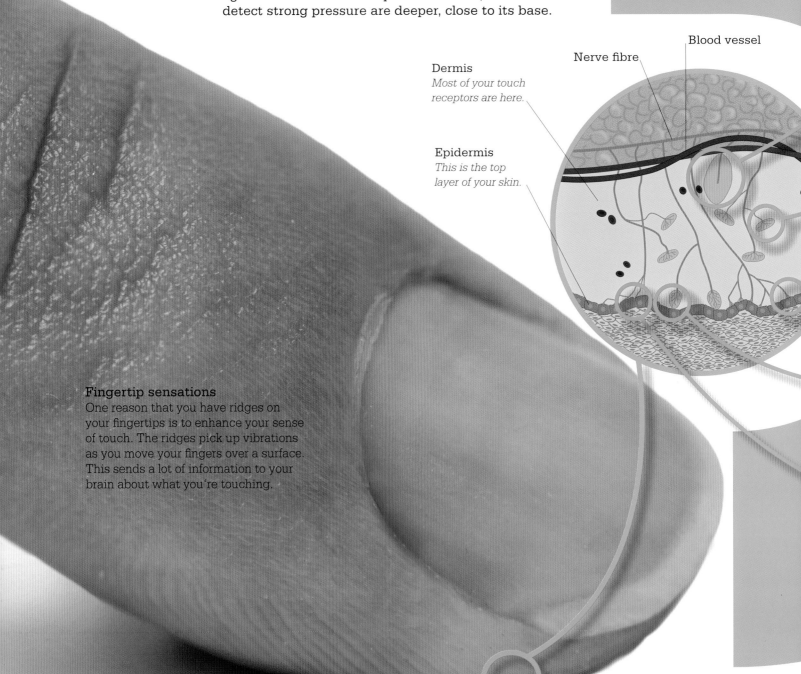

Dermis
Most of your touch receptors are here.

Epidermis
This is the top layer of your skin.

Nerve fibre

Blood vessel

Fingertip sensations
One reason that you have ridges on your fingertips is to enhance your sense of touch. The ridges pick up vibrations as you move your fingers over a surface. This sends a lot of information to your brain about what you're touching.

More or less

Your brain is very organized about how it handles touch. Your cerebral cortex (see pages 86–87) has lots of space to deal with signals from sensitive areas, such as your hands and lips, and less space to deal with signals from less sensitive parts of your body.

Pacinian corpuscles
These large receptors, each up to 1 mm (0.04 in) long, lie deep in the dermis. They detect strong touch, continued pressure, and vibrations.

Ruffini's corpuscles
Activated as the skin is stretched, these mid-dermis receptors monitor how well you are gripping an object.

Merkel's disks
At the border between the epidermis and the dermis, these react to very faint touch and pressure.

Meissner's corpuscles
Found just under the epidermis, Meissner's corpuscles detect light touch and pressure, such as gentle stroking.

Free nerve endings
Some of these reach into the epidermis. There are different nerve endings for hot and cold and for pain.

Sensitivity
More sensitive areas of the body have more receptors in the skin.

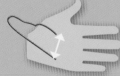

More sensitive	Less sensitive
Forehead	Shoulder
Cheek	Upper arm
Upper lip	Back
Palm	Belly
Finger	Thigh
Foot	Calf

Braille
A   B   C   D   E

Sensitive fingertips help people who are blind or whose eyesight isn't strong enough to read regular printed materials. Braille is a system of raised dots that represent letters and numbers and that are read by touch.

You have about
5,000,000
touch receptors in your skin

Why am I ticklish?
No one is certain why tickling makes us laugh. Its purpose may be to make parents and children feel emotionally closer. But we do know that some other animals, including apes and rats, are ticklish, too.

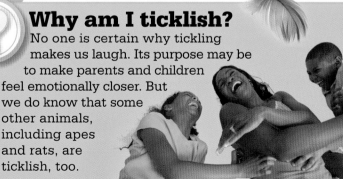

You do it!
Touch test
This test will show you which places on the body are most sensitive to touch.

0.5 IN

1 Straighten out a paper clip, then bend it into a U-shape with the ends about 1 cm (0.5 in) apart.

2 Gently press both ends of the paper clip onto the back of a friend's hand. She should keep her eyes closed.

3 If your friend feels only one point, widen the U-shape until she feels two.

4 Measure the distance between the ends of the paper clip.

5 Try different parts of your friend's body, such as her palm, ankle, or calf. The most touch-sensitive area is where she can detect the two separate points with the smallest tip separation.

Tast and sm ll [Adding

Taste and smell help us enjoy the flavours of food. In fact, smell accounts for 75–95 percent of the impact a taste has! Without smell, you might find it hard to tell a potato from a pear without looking.

How taste works

Tastes are detected by specialized nerve cells. These receptors are grouped into 10,000 clusters called taste buds. Most taste buds are on the tongue. There are also some on the throat, palate (roof of the mouth), and epiglottis.

Brain links

Cerebral cortex

Messages from the tongue travel along nerves to lower parts of the brain and then up to the cerebral cortex (see pages 86–87). Signals from the nose travel to the cortex via the limbic system (see page 87), which is linked to memory and emotion. That's why some smells remind you of past events and feelings.

Sensory centres

Signals from the tongue and nose go to special areas in the cerebral cortex for interpretation.

Limbic system inside here

The tongue and its papillae

The tongue's upper surface is covered in pimple-like projections called papillae, many of which have taste buds on them. Papillae also help your tongue grip food when you chew.

Hair-like tip

Receptor cell

Nerve fibres

Epiglottis

Foliate papillae

These papillae are leaf-like folds on the rear edges of your tongue. There are about 120 taste buds on each fold.

Fungiform papillae

Resembling miniature red mushrooms, these papillae have 3–4 taste buds each.

Taste bud

Receptor cells in taste buds have hair-like tips. These detect chemicals from food dissolved by saliva. The cells' nerve fibres relay messages to the brain to enable it to identify the tastes.

Circumvallate papillae

You have only 10 to 15 of this kind of papilla. Each has about 240 taste buds.

Filiform papillae

These papillae have no taste buds, but they help grip food.

The five basic tastes

You have receptors for sweet, sour, salty, and bitter tastes, plus a savoury taste called umami. Taste buds detect different combinations of these five tastes.

SWEET

SOUR

SALTY

BITTER

UMAMI

How smell works

Your tongue detects just 5 basic tastes, but your nose recognizes 10,000 different smells! In the roof of each of your nasal cavities is a patch the size of a thumbprint called an olfactory epithelium. Together, the two epithelia contain around 25 million smell receptors.

Olfactory bulb
Signals from smell receptors are sent from here to the brain.

Scent particle

Nostril
Scent particles enter the nasal cavities through the nostrils.

Nasal cavity
This contains mucus-covered folds, which trap pollen and dust. The folds also ensure an even airflow over the epithelia and keep them from drying out.

TO THE BRAIN

Olfactory epithelium

Smell receptor
Signals from the smell receptors travel along nerve fibres to the olfactory bulb.

Cilia
When scent molecules touch the cilia, the smell receptors fire off nerve signals.

Mucus

Olfactory epithelium
This contains smell receptors and is covered in watery mucus. Each receptor has about 20 hair-like cilia. These can detect scent particles dissolved in the mucus.

Nerve fibre

Dogs' noses are up to 100,000x more sensitive than our own

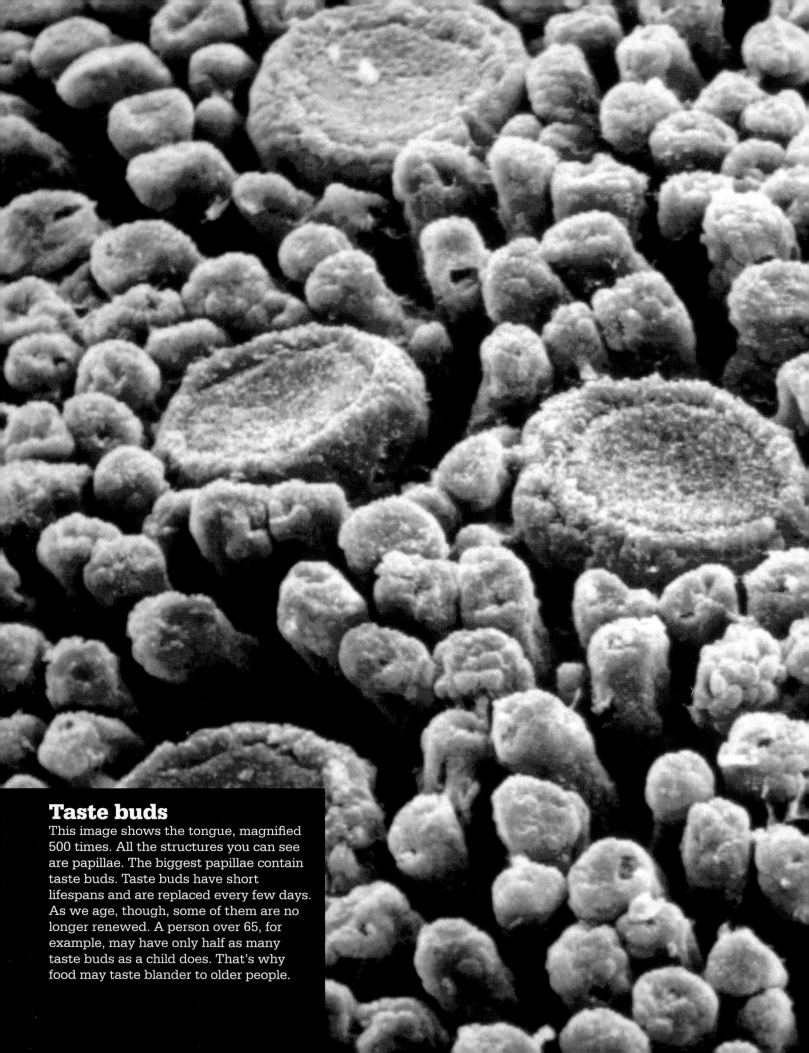

Taste buds

This image shows the tongue, magnified 500 times. All the structures you can see are papillae. The biggest papillae contain taste buds. Taste buds have short lifespans and are replaced every few days. As we age, though, some of them are no longer renewed. A person over 65, for example, may have only half as many taste buds as a child does. That's why food may taste blander to older people.

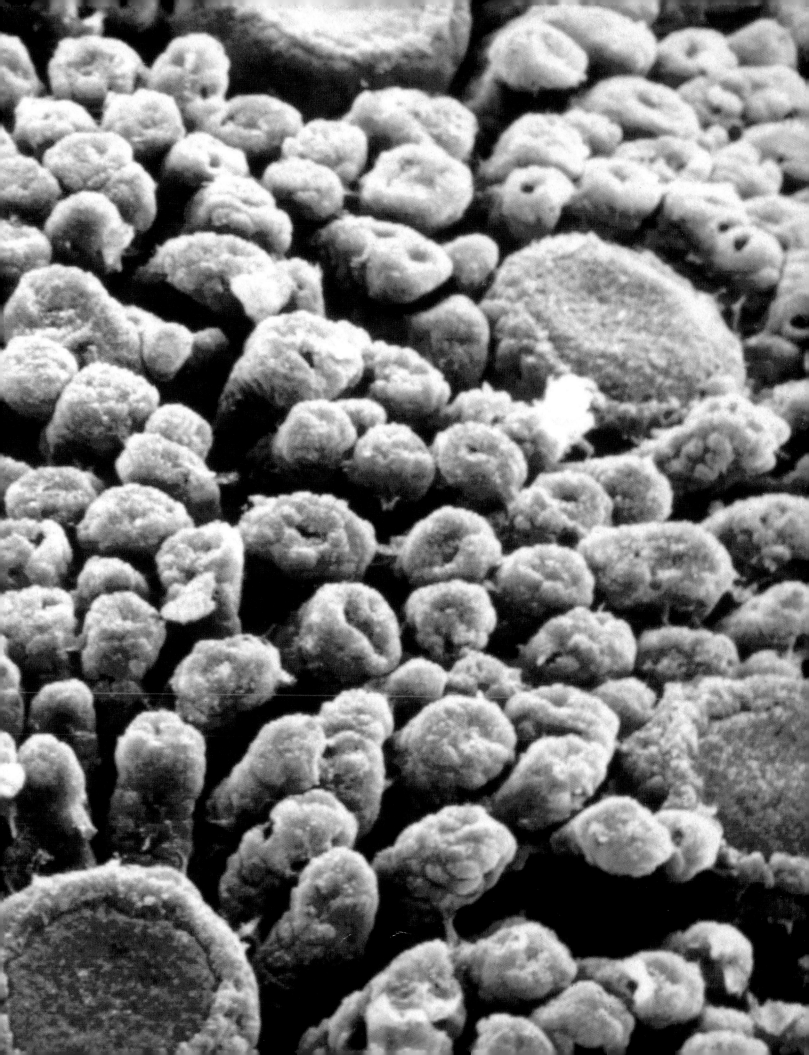

Sight [The eyes have it!]

Your eyes are your windows on the world, giving you visual information about your surroundings. At the back of each eye, a layer called the retina is packed with light-sensitive cells called rods and cones.

How you see

Light rays from an object are bent and focused by the cornea and the lens to form an upside-down image on the retina. Nerve signals travel along the optic nerve to the brain, which turns the image right side up.

Inside the eye

The eye is filled with a thick jelly called vitreous humour. The most sensitive part of the retina is called the fovea.

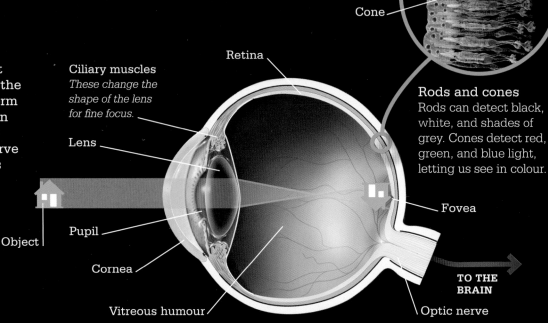

Rod

Cone

Retina

Ciliary muscles
These change the shape of the lens for fine focus.

Lens

Object

Pupil

Cornea

Vitreous humour

Rods and cones

Rods can detect black, white, and shades of grey. Cones detect red, green, and blue light, letting us see in colour.

Fovea

Optic nerve

TO THE BRAIN

In focus

The lens becomes fatter and more rounded to keep nearby objects in focus. To bring objects further away into focus, it becomes thinner and flatter.

Lens more rounded

Lens flatter

NEAR VISION

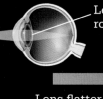

DISTANT VISION

Look sharp!

You can't see near and distant objects in focus at the same time. You have to choose which to focus on.

Binocular vision

Seeing with two eyes is called binocular vision. This gives you 3D vision and allows you to judge distances. That means you can catch and throw a ball.

Pathways

Each eye has a different view of the same object. Signals travel from the eyes to the brain. The brain creates a single 3D picture.

Right view

Left view

Eye

Optic nerves cross each other

Combined view

Visual area of brain

Why do I need glasses?

For you to see clearly, light rays must focus on your retinas. If you are near-sighted, your eyes focus light in front of your retinas, so far objects look fuzzy. If you are far-sighted, your eyes focus light behind your retinas, so close objects look fuzzy. The shapes of lenses in glasses correct the way light focuses, giving you perfect vision.

Optical illusion
The eyes can trick the brain. If you focus on
a spot outside this pattern, the pattern will
appear to rotate. This effect may be caused by
the eyes' normal rapid, irregular movements.

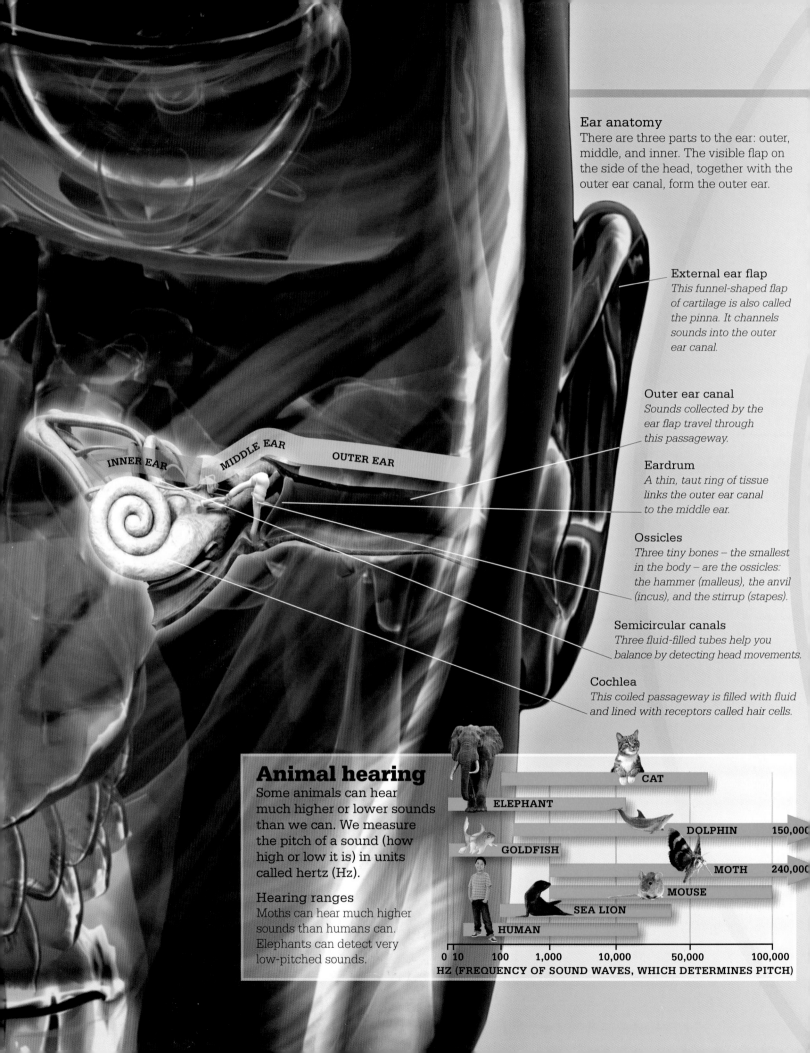

Ear anatomy
There are three parts to the ear: outer, middle, and inner. The visible flap on the side of the head, together with the outer ear canal, form the outer ear.

External ear flap
This funnel-shaped flap of cartilage is also called the pinna. It channels sounds into the outer ear canal.

Outer ear canal
Sounds collected by the ear flap travel through this passageway.

Eardrum
A thin, taut ring of tissue links the outer ear canal to the middle ear.

Ossicles
Three tiny bones – the smallest in the body – are the ossicles: the hammer (malleus), the anvil (incus), and the stirrup (stapes).

Semicircular canals
Three fluid-filled tubes help you balance by detecting head movements.

Cochlea
This coiled passageway is filled with fluid and lined with receptors called hair cells.

INNER EAR MIDDLE EAR OUTER EAR

Animal hearing
Some animals can hear much higher or lower sounds than we can. We measure the pitch of a sound (how high or low it is) in units called hertz (Hz).

Hearing ranges
Moths can hear much higher sounds than humans can. Elephants can detect very low-pitched sounds.

CAT
ELEPHANT
DOLPHIN 150,000
GOLDFISH
MOTH 240,000
MOUSE
SEA LION
HUMAN

0 10   100   1,000   10,000   50,000   100,000
HZ (FREQUENCY OF SOUND WAVES, WHICH DETERMINES PITCH)

You can hear because you have ears! And each of your ears contains organs of balance – the semicircular canals and the vestibule. Although separate, the hearing and balance organs are linked. That's why an ear infection often makes you feel dizzy.

Bats use their amazing **hearing** to listen for echoes that **help them locate** flying insects

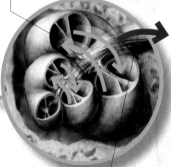

Listen up!
The ear's sound-sensing part is the snail-shaped cochlea. It contains about 15,000 sensitive hair cells. When vibrations produced by sound waves enter the ear, the hair cells send signals to the brain.

3 Shaking drum
The eardrum vibrates when struck by sound waves.

4 Vibrating bones
Vibrations from the eardrum travel along the ossicles to the inner ear.

5 Into the cochlea
The vibrations enter the fluid-filled cochlea.

Auditory nerve
This takes signals to the brain.

6 Hair cells
The vibrations produce ripples in the cochlea's fluid. The ripples stimulate the hair cells to fire off nerve signals.

1 Sound in
Waves of vibrations in the air enter the ear.

2 Waves
Sound waves travel up the outer ear canal.

Eustachian tube
This connects to the throat.

7 To the brain
Nerve signals from the hair cells zoom along the auditory nerve to the brain, which analyzes the sound.

Vestibular nerve
This sends signals to the brain.

Semicircular canals
These are at right angles to one another. They detect motion in three directions, one per canal.

Vestibule
This monitors the head's position.

Balancing
The semicircular canals and the vestibule help you balance. They are filled with fluid and cells with tiny hairs. When you move your head, the fluid moves and bends the hairs. The movement of the hairs causes the cells to send messages to your brain. Your brain tells your body how to stay balanced.

Balance organs
It's not only your semicircular canals and vestibule that help you balance. Information from your eyes, your muscles, and pressure receptors in your skin (see pages 90–91) is also important.

Why don't ballet dancers get dizzy?
If you turn rapidly, the fluid in your balance organs keeps moving even after you stop. This movement can make you feel like you are spinning. Dancers avoid this dizziness by turning their heads rapidly to keep staring at a fixed point while their bodies spin more slowly.

DNA [The molecule of life]

DNA is your body's blueprint. Molecules of DNA are tucked away inside the nuclei of your cells. They contain instructions, in the form of genes, that keep your body alive and kicking.

Unravelling DNA

If all the DNA molecules in a cell were laid end to end, they would stretch for 2 m (6.6 ft). Each DNA molecule twists and coils itself into a compact structure called a chromosome. It untwists into a ladder-like shape.

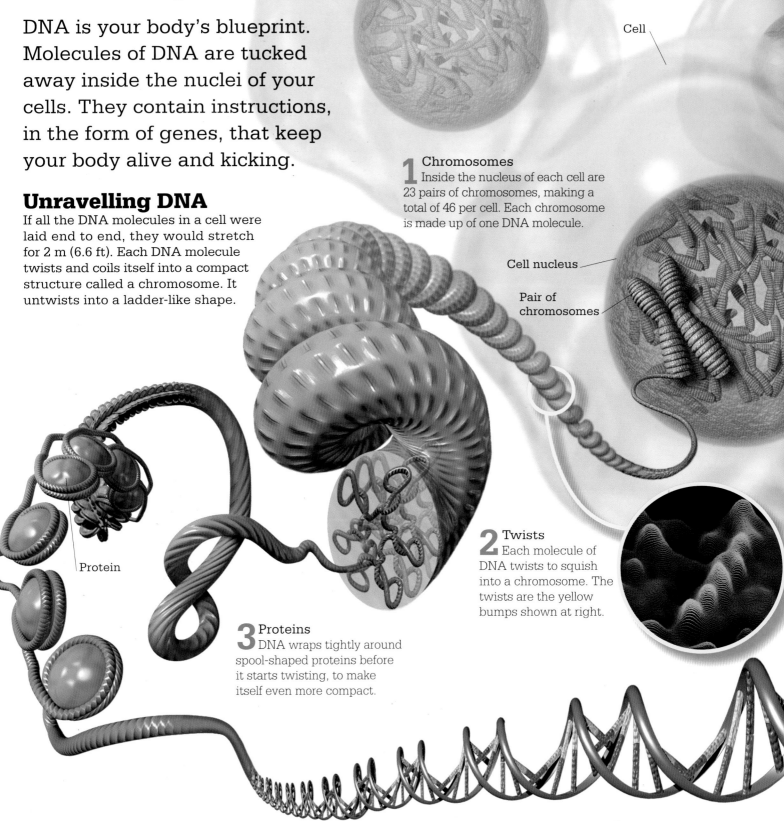

Cell

1 Chromosomes
Inside the nucleus of each cell are 23 pairs of chromosomes, making a total of 46 per cell. Each chromosome is made up of one DNA molecule.

Cell nucleus

Pair of chromosomes

Protein

2 Twists
Each molecule of DNA twists to squish into a chromosome. The twists are the yellow bumps shown at right.

3 Proteins
DNA wraps tightly around spool-shaped proteins before it starts twisting, to make itself even more compact.

If unravelled, a human's DNA would stretch to the Sun and back more than 200 times

DNA milestones

By 1952, scientists understood a lot about how DNA works. But they didn't know exactly what shape it was or how genes were arranged in it. In the last 60 years, scientists have worked out DNA's shape. They have also discovered that there are approximately 20,000–25,000 human genes, and what many of them do.

First images, 1952
Rosalind Franklin used X-rays to produce images that hinted at DNA's shape.

DNA model, 1953
James Watson and Francis Crick created a model of DNA's structure.

Gene map, 2003
Scientists finished working out how all human genes are arranged.

More = better?

Only a small amount of DNA is used for genes (1.5 percent in humans). Much of the rest, called junk DNA, has no known purpose. So having more chromosomes, or more DNA, doesn't make an organism more complex.

Species compared
A human has fewer chromosomes than an adder's-tongue fern does!

ADDER'S-TONGUE	AFRICAN HEDGEHOG	HUMAN	JACK JUMPER ANT
1,260 chromosomes	**88** chromosomes	**46** chromosomes	**2** chromosomes

Genes

A gene is a section of DNA that contains a code that tells your body what to do. The code is in the form of bases, or paired chemicals. There are four bases: adenine, cytosine, guanine, and thymine, or A, C, G, and T for short. A string of these bases in a certain order – a gene – controls a particular cell activity or the production of a particular protein.

Passed to you

Genes control the production of all the proteins in your body. Proteins are involved in how you develop and function. You inherit your genes from your parents. That's why you are like them in many ways.

4 Two strands
Untwisted, DNA reveals that it is made of two strands. Chemical links between the two are like rungs on a ladder.

Adenine (A) Guanine (G) Thymine (T) Cytosine (C)

A T G A C G G A T C A G C
T A C T G C C T A G T C G

Holding it all together
The twin strands, made from sugar and phosphate, are the "backbones" of the molecule.

Matching pairs
The base chemicals always pair up in the same ways – A with T, and C with G. Your DNA contains 3.2 billion base pairs. Each gene contains, on average, 27,000 of these chemical pairings.

Family connections
Turn the page to find out how the genes you inherited make you you!

Inheritance [Genes, not jeans]

Have you ever wondered why your eyes are the colour they are, or why your hair is curly or straight? It's all up to your genes. The way you look and the way your body is put together are the result of the genes that you inherited from your parents.

How did I get my genes?

You inherited 23 chromosomes, with their genes, from your mother and 23 chromosomes, with their genes, from your father. Your parents, in turn, inherited their genes from their parents – your grandparents. You, your parents, and your grandparents each ended up with 23 pairs of chromosomes, 46 in total.

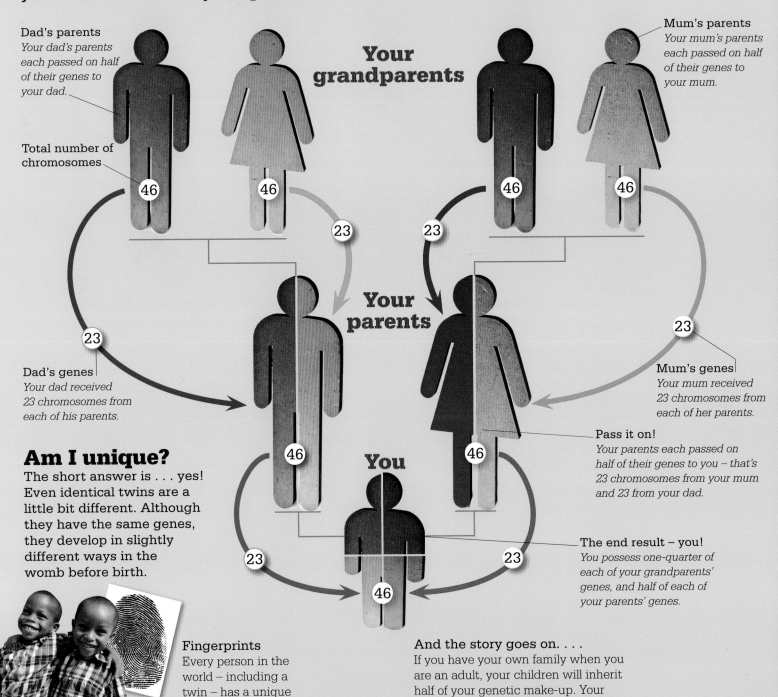

Dad's parents
Your dad's parents each passed on half of their genes to your dad.

Mum's parents
Your mum's parents each passed on half of their genes to your mum.

Your grandparents

Total number of chromosomes

Your parents

Dad's genes
Your dad received 23 chromosomes from each of his parents.

Mum's genes
Your mum received 23 chromosomes from each of her parents.

Pass it on!
Your parents each passed on half of their genes to you – that's 23 chromosomes from your mum and 23 from your dad.

You

The end result – you!
You possess one-quarter of each of your grandparents' genes, and half of each of your parents' genes.

Am I unique?

The short answer is . . . yes! Even identical twins are a little bit different. Although they have the same genes, they develop in slightly different ways in the womb before birth.

Fingerprints
Every person in the world – including a twin – has a unique set of fingerprints.

And the story goes on. . . .
If you have your own family when you are an adult, your children will inherit half of your genetic make-up. Your grandchildren will inherit one-quarter.

Boy or girl

Your 23rd pair of chromosomes determines your sex – whether you are a girl or a boy. A girl has two X chromosomes; a boy has one X and one Y chromosome.

X + X = ♀ GIRL

X + Y = ♂ BOY

Strong or weak

The genes of each pair of chromosomes determine something about you – for example, the colour of your hair or eyes. Sometimes one of the genes is stronger than the other. The stronger gene is described as dominant, while the weaker gene is described as recessive.

X-linked gene

Red-green colour blindness is caused by a faulty recessive gene on the X chromosome. Women are not often affected, because a healthy gene in their second X chromosome will dominate the faulty gene.

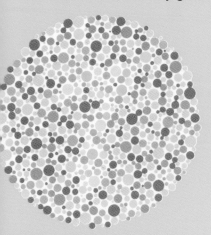

Colour blindness test
Red and green look the same to some people. Can you see a number hidden in this circle?

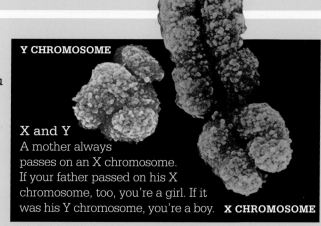

Y CHROMOSOME

X and Y
A mother always passes on an X chromosome. If your father passed on his X chromosome, too, you're a girl. If it was his Y chromosome, you're a boy. **X CHROMOSOME**

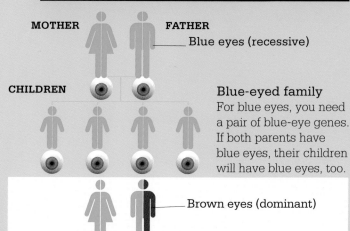

MOTHER · FATHER
Blue eyes (recessive)

CHILDREN

Blue-eyed family
For blue eyes, you need a pair of blue-eye genes. If both parents have blue eyes, their children will have blue eyes, too.

Brown eyes (dominant)

50-50
If one parent has one brown-eye gene, each child has a 50-50 chance of having brown eyes.

Probably brown
If each parent has one blue-eye gene and one brown-eye gene, they both have brown eyes. Each child has a 75 percent chance of having brown eyes.

Brown-eyed kids
If one parent has only blue genes and the other has only brown, their children will definitely have brown eyes. Brown will always dominate.

What else did you inherit?

There is a lot more to inheritance than eye and hair colour. Here are a few traits you might not realize you inherited. How many others in your family share these traits?

ABILITY TO ROLL TONGUE

BENT PINKY FINGER

DIMPLES

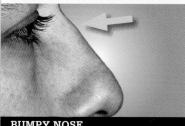

BUMPY NOSE

FRECKLES

Growing up

How much have you changed since your last birthday? Probably a lot! As a newborn baby, you were tiny and totally helpless. But every year you will grow and change, especially during your teens.

Getting bigger

In your first 6 months, you doubled in weight. By the age of 2, you doubled your weight again. Then you grow steadily until a major growth spurt at the start of puberty. This is when hormones released by your body trigger changes that mean you are becoming an adult.

Newborn baby

When you are not being fed, you are mostly sleeping – about 16 hours a day! You cannot control your movements. You can focus only on nearby objects.

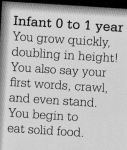

Infant 0 to 1 year

You grow quickly, doubling in height! You also say your first words, crawl, and even stand. You begin to eat solid food.

A baby's brain makes 2 million new synapse

Child 3 to 6

Your language skills improve. You express feelings – sometimes with tantrums! You learn to play with other children. And you begin to draw and form letters.

Child 6 to 8

You tackle complex movements, such as playing sports. Your thinking is more logical, and you can solve problems. You may start to lose your baby teeth.

Teething time

When you were born, there were 20 milk teeth inside your jaw. They didn't start to break through your gums until you were a few months old. The milk teeth are gradually replaced by 32 adult teeth as you grow.

Milk teeth

Adult teeth

Move over!
Your milk teeth loosen and fall out as your adult teeth grow beneath them. Call the tooth fairy!

Toddler 1 to 2
Your muscles are stronger. You learn to walk, climb stairs, and carry things. By age 2, your brain is about 80 percent of its adult size.

Toddler 2 to 3
Muscle control is better, so you can turn a book's pages, build brick towers, scribble, and feed yourself – messily! You can say 250 to 900 words.

neuron connections) every second

Child 8 to 12
You can now write stories and do math. You like having friends. Hormones begin to change your body from about age 10. You may start to grow adult body hair.

Teenager 12 to 18
Hormones change your body a lot. Boys' voices drop and their muscles get bigger. Girls begin to develop curves. Sweating, acne, and body odour can be problems.

adrenaline
A hormone that gets the body ready to react to stress or danger.

alveolus
One of many tiny air sacs in the lungs where gases are exchanged between air and blood. The plural of *alveolus* is *alveoli*.

antibiotic
A medical drug that either kills harmful bacteria that have infected the body or keeps them from multiplying.

antibody
A chemical made by the body's immune system to disable invading germs or mark them for destruction.

artery
A thick-walled blood vessel that carries fresh blood from the heart to tissues and organs.

atrium
One of the heart's two upper chambers. The plural of *atrium* is *atria*.

axon
The long "tail" of a neuron, which carries signals away from the cell body. An axon is also called a nerve fibre.

bacterium
A simple, microscopic life-form made up of only one cell. Bacteria are the most abundant form of life on Earth. The plural of *bacterium* is *bacteria*.

blood clot
A mesh made of trapped red blood cells that forms when a blood vessel is damaged.

bone
A hard tissue that gives strength to the skeleton. Bone is made chiefly of the minerals calcium and phosphorus.

bone marrow
A soft tissue inside bones. Red marrow forms blood cells, while yellow marrow stores fat.

capillary
One of the microscopic blood vessels that connect the smallest arteries with the smallest veins.

carbohydrate
An energy-rich chemical that contains carbon, hydrogen, and oxygen. Starch and sugars, such as glucose, are carbohydrates.

cardiac muscle
A type of muscle found only in the heart. It contracts and relaxes automatically, and it never tires.

cartilage
A tough, flexible tissue that covers the ends of bones in joints. It also makes up the ear flaps, the larynx, and parts of the nose.

cell
One of the tiny units that make up all living things.

cerebral cortex
The cerebrum's wrinkled surface.

cerebrum
The largest and most complex part of the brain, involved in emotions and conscious thought. It also controls movements.

chromosome
A tiny package of information, in the form of DNA, found in the nuclei of cells. Each cell in your body (except red blood cells) has 46 chromosomes.

cilium
A tiny hair-like structure found on certain body cells. The plural of *cilium* is *cilia*.

computed tomography (CT)
A technique that uses X-rays and a computer to create images that show "slices" of the body.

cornea
The clear layer at the front of the eye that allows in light.

cytoplasm
The jelly-like fluid inside a cell.

dendrite
A tentacle-like projection on the cell body of a neuron. It receives nerve signals from other cells.

dermis
The thicker layer of skin, beneath the epidermis. The dermis contains blood vessels, receptors, hair follicles, and sweat glands.

dissect
To cut open a dead animal or plant to study its internal structure.

DNA
A molecule that makes up each of the body's chromosomes and stores information. Each DNA molecule consists of two strands that spiral around each other like a twisted ladder.

dominant gene
The stronger of two different genes that carry instructions for the same characteristic, such as eye colour. If a dominant gene is paired with a weaker recessive gene, the recessive gene's effects are always masked, or hidden.

enzyme
A substance that speeds up chemical reactions, such as those that break down food during digestion.

epidermis
The tough, waterproof top layer of skin, above the dermis.

The dead, scaly cells at its surface are made of keratin.

epiglottis
A flap of cartilage at the back of the larynx. It is usually open, to let air into the lungs. It folds forwards as you swallow, to send

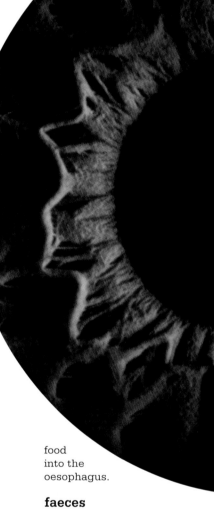

food into the oesophagus.

faeces
Semi-solid waste from digested food. Faeces are often called poo.

Glossary

follicle
A pit in the skin, out of which a hair grows. There are follicles all over the skin, except for on the lips, the palms of the hands, and the soles of the feet.

gene
The basic unit of inheritance. A gene is a section of DNA that carries all the instructions needed to make a particular protein.

germ
A microscopic organism, such as a bacterium or virus.

gland
A tissue or organ that releases chemicals, such as hormones or sweat, into or onto the body.

haemoglobin
A protein in red blood cells that contains iron and carries oxygen around the body.

hormone
A substance, released into the blood by glands, that acts as a chemical messenger.

keratin
A tough, waterproof protein found in skin, hair, and nails.

larynx
The part of the respiratory tract that contains the vocal cords, which vibrate as air passes over them to create sounds.

lens
A curved structure in the eye, made of transparent protein. The lens bends light rays entering the eye, focussing them to form an image on the retina.

ligament
A band of tough tissue that holds bones together at joints.

lymphocyte
A type of white blood cell that plays an important role in the body's immune system.

magnetic resonance imaging (MRI)
A technique that uses magnetism and radio waves to produce images of the inside of the body.

mineral
A substance, such as calcium, that we get from food to keep our bodies healthy. Many enzymes need minerals in order to function.

mitochondrion
A structure in a cell that releases energy from sugars and fats. The plural of *mitochondrion* is *mitochondria*.

mitosis
The process in which a cell divides to make two new, identical cells.

molecule
A chemical unit made up of two or more atoms joined together.

mucus
A thick fluid that protects and lubricates. Mucus is made in the respiratory and digestive systems.

muscle
A tissue that contracts in order to make a body part move. There are three types of muscle: cardiac, skeletal, and smooth.

nephron
A unit of cells inside the kidneys that filter blood and make urine.

nerve
A bundle of neurons that relays nerve signals between the central nervous system (the brain and spinal cord) and the body.

neuron
A type of cell found in the brain, the spinal cord, and nerves. Neurons carry high-speed electrical signals. A neuron is also called a nerve cell.

nucleus
A cell's control centre. It contains all the instructions needed to build the cell and keep it alive. The plural of *nucleus* is *nuclei*.

oesophagus
The muscular tube through which food passes from the pharynx to the stomach.

organ
A major body part, such as the liver, heart, or lungs, with a particular role. An organ is made up of two or more types of tissue.

organelle
A structure that has a specific role in maintaining a cell. A mitochondrion is an organelle.

osteoblast
A type of cell that builds bones.

osteoclast
A type of cell that breaks down bones.

CLOSE-UP
OF AN EYE

You are 1 cm (0.4 in) shorter in the evening than you are in the morning, because the cartilage in your spine compresses during the day

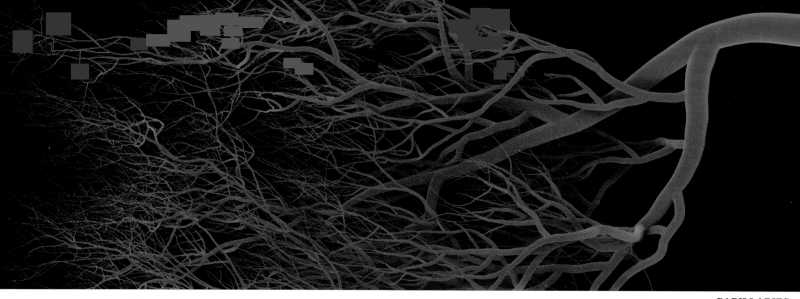

phagocyte
A white blood cell that surrounds and digests unwanted matter, such as invading germs.

pharynx
The tube that runs from the nasal cavity to the oesophagus. The pharynx is also called the throat.

plasma
The watery part of blood. It is a yellowish liquid that contains dissolved substances, such as nutrients and proteins.

platelet
A flat cell fragment found in blood. Platelets help blood clot. They clump and stick together to patch wounds in small blood vessels.

protein
A nutrient used by the body for growth and repair.

receptor
A nerve cell, or group of nerve cells, that detects changes in the body's surroundings and sends nerve signals to the brain.

recessive gene
The weaker of two different genes that carry instructions for the same characteristic, such as eye colour.

It has an effect only if it is paired with another recessive gene.

retina
A thin layer at the back of the eye that is packed with light-sensitive receptors called rods and cones.

sebum
An oily substance, made by glands in the skin, that keeps skin soft and flexible.

skeletal muscle
The type of muscle that is attached to bones. It contracts and relaxes to move the body.

smooth muscle
The type of muscle found in the walls of hollow organs, such as the bladder and small intestine. Smooth muscle contracts slowly and rhythmically.

synapse
A space between two neurons, where they come very close to each other but do not touch.

synovial joint
A freely moving joint, such as the knee or wrist. A synovial joint is lubricated by an oily liquid called synovial fluid, to reduce wear and tear on bones.

taste bud
A receptor on the surface of the tongue that detects different tastes in food and drink.

tendon
A tough cord or sheet that links muscle to bone. It transmits the force exerted by the muscle.

thalamus
The part of the brain that receives and processes information from the senses.

tissue
A collection of similar cells that work together to perform a specific task in the body.

trachea
The tube that carries air into and out of the lungs. It runs from the larynx to the bronchi. The trachea is also called the windpipe.

ultrasound
A technique that sends sound waves into the body and forms images by analyzing the echoes that bounce back.

ultraviolet (UV) ray
A type of radiation, found in sunlight. Too much exposure

to UV rays can be harmful.

urine
Waste liquid produced by the kidneys. Urine is often called pee.

vein
A thin-walled blood vessel that carries used blood from tissues and organs back to the heart.

ventricle
One of the heart's two lower chambers.

vertebra
One of the bones that make up the body's spine. The plural of *vertebra* is *vertebrae*.

virus
The tiniest form of germ. A virus takes over the cells of a living organism to make copies of itself.

vitamin
A naturally occurring chemical that the body needs in small amounts in order to stay healthy.

X-ray
A type of radiation. X-rays can be beamed through the body onto photographic film to produce images of hard body parts, such as bones.

Index

123RF/Achim Prill: 102 br; Alamy Images: 28 r, 41 main (Mike Kemp/Tetra Images), cover main (Pixologicstudio/Science Photo Library), 10, 11, 106, 107 (Suren Manvelyan); AP Images: 78 l, 89 tr (Ibrahim Usta), 42 r, 49 br (Seth Wenig); Christina Saenz de Santamaria: 67; Clive Streeter: 90 l; Dreamstime: 58 tapeworms (3drenderings), 49 t, 101 tr (Alila07), 82 main, 83 bg (Amuzica), 53 blood drop (Ayzek09), 91 lt (Convit), 17 teeth (Deyangeorgiev), 31 b (Glenda Powers), 103 rt (Joshua Wanyama), 52 b, 53 b (London_England), back cover screen (Manaemedia), 103 rct (R. Gino Santa Maria), 91 rt (Red2000), 17 pancreas, 17 thyroid gland (Sebastian Kaulitzki), 35 b (Serrnovik), 87 t (Shubhangi Kene), 103 lb (Siraanamwong), 96 bl (Tru9ja), 93 bg (Yuri Arcurs); Emma Forge: 45 tr; Fotolia: 72 food (afxhome), 72 food (alexlukin), 72 food (Andrey Starostin), 72 food (Anna Kucherova), 72 food (Antonio Gravante), 72 food (Aygul Bulté), 72 food (bergamont), 72 food (Brad Pict), 72 food (crspix), 72 food (Denis Gladkiy), 72 food (Diana Taliun), 72 food (Digitalpress), 72 food (Dionisvera), 72 food (dream79), 72 food (Edward Westmacott), 72 food (EM Art), 72 food (Fotofermer), 72 food (fotyma), 72 food (Giuseppe Porzani), 72 food (Givaga), 72 food (gmeviphoto), 72 food (goodween123), 72 food (Ian 2010), 72 food (indigolotos), 72 food (Jarp), 72 food (Joe Gough), 72 food (juliedeshaies), 72 food (karandaev), 72 food (kostrez), 72 food (lefebvre_jonathan), 72 food (Leonid Nyshko), 72 food (lom66), 72 food (Marek), 72 food (margo555), 72 food (marylooo), 72 food (mayakova), 72 food (MediablitzImages), 72 food (mericozkaya), 72 food (michelangelus), 72 food (monropic), 72 food (monticellllo), 72 food (Natalia Mylova), 72 food (Natika), 72 food (Nikolay Pozdeyev), 72 food (nito), 72 food (Okea), 72 food (Only Fabrizio), 72 food (phasinphoto), 72 food (photocrew), 72 food (pixbox77), 72 food (ppi09), 72 food (Remains), 72 food (Sergio Martínez), 72 food (sommai), 72 food (stoleg), 72 food (Subbotina Anna), 72 food (SunnyS), 72 food (Thongchai Pittayanon), 72 food (Tim UR), 72 food (torsakarin), 72 food (Viktor), 72 food (womue); Getty Images: 27 b, 27 tl, 27 tr (Dr. Richard Kessel & Dr. Gene Shih), 8, 9 (Helene Wiesenhaan), 62 bg main, 63 bg main (MedicalRF.com), 16 sweat glands, 16 sebaceous gland, 44 br (Science Picture Co); iStockphoto: 89 tl (2happy), 74 c (3drenderings), 73 drumstick (4kodiak), 44 strongman (AdrianHillman), 58 viruses (adventtr), 75 br, 75 br inset (aguirre_mar), 16 alveoli, 16 ligaments, 39 joints, 40 lb (alex-mit), 17 cochlea, 17 semicircular canals (alexluengo), 73 salmon (AlexStar), 98 mouse (alptraum), 105 ctl (andipantz), 72 yogurt (AndreyTTL), 14 cbr, 16 heart, 39 b white icons, 40 lt (angelhell), 59 stings, 87 bee, 98 moth (Antagain), 88 ct, 89 heart art (AnvilArtworks), 24 cl (AptTone), 96 cr (atiatiati), 73 bc (Auke Holwerda), 39 b black icons, 48 l icons (Barbulat), 48 t border, 48 l border, 49 t border, 49 r border (Barcin), 12 c, 26 br (BeholdingEye), 104 screens, 105 screens (Big_Ryan), 104 tl (bluehill75), 73 raspberries (bluestocking), 73 sausage (BrianAJackson), 96 tl (browndogstudios), 16 skin (chaoss), 16 lungs (comotion_design), 30 main, 31 c (cosmin4000), 92 bitter (creativepictures), 72 broccoli (Creativeye99), 17 liver, 17 small intestine (CreVis2), 105 tl (cujo19), 24 cr (CurvaBezier), 25 tl (D4Fish), 7 cr, 17 thymus gland, 35 tl (David Marchal), 99 br (DaydreamsGirl), 17 gallbladder, 17 limbic system, 52 b heart, 56 lt (decade3d), 73 t-bone steak (Diane Labombarbe), 59 antibodies (Dimitris66), 72 broccoli (Dizzy), 4 brains, 5 brains, 72 zucchini, 87 t brain (DNY59), back cover heart (Dorling_Kindersley), cover red cells, 25 cr, 26 bl (DTKUTOO), 73 t-bone steak (DustyPixel), 92 salty (edelmar), 58 cl (EduardHarkonen), 72 asparagus (egal), 73 pomegranates (eli_asenova), 16 white blood cell, 26 bcl, 53 white blood cells, 58 bacteria (Eraxion), 72 leeks (evemilla), 33 br (fatchoi), 16 nail (firebrandphotography), 72 leek, 72 cucumber, 72 asparagus, 72 romaine lettuce, 72 lollo bionda, 73 roast chicken, 92 sweet (Floortje), 72 peas (FuatKose), 103 rb (Funwithfood), 73 currant (Gabor Izso), 17 retina (Gannet77), 56 bg, 57 bg (gimbat), 59 cats, 87 chimp, 98 sea lion (GlobalP), 16 tendon (goa_novi), 72 plum (GooDween123), 59 nickel in jewelry (graytown), 72 cucumber (Hors), 69 bl (Ian McDonnell), 72 food (Ildi_Papp), 17 bladder, 35 tr, 103 boy symbol (IngramPublishing), 52 tr, 108 (Inok), 68 l (IPGGutenbergUKLtd), 98 goldfish (Irochka_T), 104 cbc (isitsharp), 73 raspberries (ivanmateev), 104 bl (jallfree), 105 tc (Jani Bryson), 17 salivary glands, 17 olfactory bulb, 17 pituitary gland (janulla), 105 cbr (jaroon), 16 skull (JazzIRT), 72 green pepper (jerryhat), 58 ct (Jodi Jacobson), 73 ribeye (JoeGough), 72 cereal bowl (joeygil), 98 human (Johnny Greig), 59 peanuts (Kaan Ates), 104 tc (Kali Nine LLC), 104 bc, 104 br (kate_sept2004), 48 r bg (Kevin Landwer-Johan), 57 b (kosziv), 73 bl (KristianSeptimiusKrogh), 101 male icon, 101 female icon, 102 male icon, 102 female icon, 103 male icon, 103 female icon (leminuit), 73 pears (lindilu), 101 b (Lokibaho), 17 kidneys, 35 tc, 40 hinge joint, 40 gliding joint (London_England), 73 br (LPETTET), 104 ctc (macniak), 72 fried egg (malerapaso), 73 sausage (mariusFM77), 73 strawberry (MariuszBlach), 87 b brain (Medical Art Inc), 96 cl (meltonmedia), 87 boy (michaeljung), 44 thermometer (mikemcd), 72 cabbage (morningarage), 44 bl (MrPlumo), 73 red plum (Natikka), 17 eyes (Neustockimages), 104 ctr (Ni Qin), 58 cr (nico_blue), 69 bcl, 105 ctr inset r, 105 cbl (nicolesy), 59 pollen (NNehring), 72 bcl (Ockra), 17 iris (ODV), 89 br (Oktay Ortakcioglu), 80 b, 105 ctr (onebluelight), 72 yogurt (OxfordSquare), 73 salmon (paci77), 72 pasta (parfyonov), 24 l (paulprescott72), 59 cosmetics (pederk), 33 bl (petesaloutos), 89 muscle art (philhol), 45 tl inset (photochecker), 72 strawberry yogurt (Photoevent), 73 cherries (photomaru), 93 smoke (piccerella), 104 cbr (PicturePartners), 17 brain (Pitton), 73 pears (pixhook), 17 touch receptors (pixologicstudio), 73 sausage (prapassong), 73 r icons (pringletta), 25 bcl (pxhidalgo), 73 tr, 73 tl (rangepuppies), 105 cbc (ranplett), 72 butterhead lettuce, 92 sour (RedHelga), 44 sunglasses (roccomontoya), 73 raspberries (roman_sh), 89 tc (RTimages), 73 drumstick (Saddako), 103 girl symbol (Samarskaya), 73 r icons (sasimoto), 17 tongue (sdominick), 17 neuron (sgame), 105 br (shironosov), 58 cb (Smithore), cover blue cells, 59 rc, 59 rt (somersault18:24), 72 sour cream (Stepan Popov), 104 cbl (Steve Debenport), 72 peas (stocknshares), 25 cl (Studio-Annika), 72 kale (Suzifoo), 17 large intestine (t.light), 98 elephant (Taalvi), 25 bcr (Tsuji), 73 red apple (Turnervisual), 63 b (ultrapro), 104 tr (video1), 105 bl (Vikram Raghuvanshi), 73 mango (Viktor Lugovskoy), 104 ctl (visiblelight), 98 cat (WebSubstance), 53 t (wellglad), 98 dolphin (Witthaya), 105 ctr inset l, 105 ctr inset cl (wsphotos), 103 eyeballs (Xacto), 25 bl, 72 bl, 73 eggs (YinYang), 105 ctr inset cr (YouraPechkin), 49 l bg (Yuri_Arcurs), 25 tr (ZargonDesign), 72 artichoke (ZoneCreative); Scholastic, Inc.: 14 t, 39 tc; Science Photo Library: 101 tc (A. Barrington Brown), 49 bc (Anatomical Travelogue), 16 nasal passages, 16 vocal cords, 17 pharynx, 68 r, 69 tl (Claus Lunau), 69 tr (Dr Gary Settles), 23 lb (Du Cane Medical Imaging Ltd), 92 t (Fernando Da Cunha/BSIP), 1 (Gustoimages), 16 bone marrow, 38 t, 78 c, 86, 92 clt, 92 c, 100 main (Henning Dalhoff), 93 b (Jacopin), 22 rb (Juergen Berger), 88 cl (Lawrence Lawry), 18 l (Medi-Mation), 88 bl (NIBSC), 23 r, 26 tr (Pasieka), 12 r, 23 cb (Philippe Psaila), 74 br, 87 bl (Pixologicstudio), 38 bl, 46 inset (Power and Syred), 101 tl (Science Source), 7 cl, 28 c, 39 tl, 42 c, 46 main, 48 br, 49 c, 78 r, 84, 85, 88 crb (Steve Gschmeissner), 2, 3, 50 l, 53 cr, 54, 55 (Susumu Nishinaga), 47 (Thierry Berrod, Mona Lisa Production); Science Source: 56 main heart, 63 tl, 92 clb, 98 bg, 99 cl (3D4Medical), 45 c, 45 cr (Adam Hart-Davis), 91 lc, 99 cr (Anatomical Travelogue), 42 l, 43 t bg, 44 t bg (Andrew Syred), 16 epiglottis (Annaïck Kermoal), 75 cb (ASM/Jessica Wilson), 99 t (B. G. Thomson), 22 rc, 39 c, 39 bl, 44 bc, 91 lb (Biophoto Associates), 103 lt (Biophoto Associates/Robin Treadwell), 26 tl, 32 bl, 59 tr, 74 bg, 74 t, 75 bg, 105 tr (BSIP), 59 tcr (Carol and Mike Werner), 24 r (Charles D. Winters), 45 tl, 58 bc (Clouds Hill Imaging Ltd.), 77 b (David M. Phillips/Jessica Wilson), 26 cl, 77 t (David M. Phillips/Mary Martin), 58 bl (David Mack), 16 larynx, 16 trachea, 16 bronchi, 62 bg inset, 63 bg inset (David Marchal), 23 ct (Dr. Najeeb Layyous), 45 cl, 48 c, 49 bl, 62 br, 62 t, 75 tr (Eye of Science), 96 tc (Jacopin), 76 main, 77 bg (James Cavallini), 58 fungi, 81 b (Manfred Kage), 6, 17 taste buds, 92 crb, 94, 95 (Mary Martin), 12 l, 14 cbl, 17 esophagus, 18 cl, 18 cr, 18 r, 19 r, 19 cr, 19 l, 19 cl, 34 ct, 34 b, 35 t, 35 cb, 40 ball-and-socket joint (Medi-Mation), 14 b, 14 bg, 15 bg (Medi-Mation Ltd/SPL), 99 bl (MedicalRF), 81 tc (Microscape), 59 c (NIBSC), 81 tr (P. Motta), 17 rods and cones, 59 tclt, 59 tclb, 59 tl, 96 tr (Pasieka), 14 ctl (Pasieka/SPL), 39 tr (Paul Gunning), 40 inset joints (Peter Gardiner), 80 bg, 81 bg (Pixologicstudio/SPL), 92 crc (Prof. P.M. Motta/Univ. "La Sapienza", Rome), 26 cr (Quest), 59 rb, 88 crt, 88 tr (Roger Harris), 7 l, 22 ct (Sheila Terry), 26 bcr, 28 l, 39 br, 57 tl, 58 br, 80 t, 97 (SPL), 17 nerves, 56 lb, 81 tl (Steve Gschmeissner), 7 r, 57 cl, 65 r, 75 tc (Susumu Nishinaga), 38 br (Ted Kinsman), 75 ct, 14 cr (Thomas Deerinck, NCMIR/SPL), 50 r, 58 protozoa, 60, 61, 92 crt, 100 inset; Shutterstock, Inc.: 70 r, 77 c (abstractdesignlabs), 17 pineal gland (Alex Luengo), 17 eardrum, 62 bl, 63 tr, 65 cb, 74 bc, 96 br (Alila Medical Media), 65 t (Andrea Danti), 16 compact bone (BioMedical), 16 artery, 16 capillaries, 16 skeletal muscle, 16 vein, 52 tl (BlueRingMedia), 17 optic nerve (CLIPAREA l Custom media), 16 hair follicle (dream designs), 75 bc (dream designs), 25 br (Ed Isaacs), 102 bl (Felix Mizioznikov), 17 stomach (Graphic Compressor), 57 cr (GRei), 16 synovial joint, 23 ltr (itsmejust), 75 bl (Lightspring), 17 mouth (Malyugin), 17 cornea (Michal Vitek), 74 bl (milias1987), 16 red blood cells (monika3steps), 17 parathyroid glands (O2creationz), 52 c (Pan Xunbin), 69 br, 70 c, 75 tl (PathDoc), 17 pupil (Phatic-Photography), 58 tr (Pressmaster), 65 ctc (Samuel Borges Photography), 17 ear (schankz), 40 pivot joint, 53 blood parts, 88 br (Sebastian Kaulitzki), 69 bcr (Sergey Furtaev), 104 bg, 105 bg (spirit of america), 50 c, 66 (Taras Kushnir), 65 ctl, 65 ctr (Yoko Design), 16 spongy bone (zimowa); Thinkstock: 103 rcb (adrian stewart roberts), 88 tl (Cathy Yeulet), 91 rb (ERproductions Ltd), 103 rc (Jani Bryson), 88 bc (karelnoppe), 22 rtr (Lion Hijmans); Tim Loughhead/Precision Illustration: 32 b bg, 32 soccer player, 33 b bg, 33 soccer player, 33 l illustration, 33 r illustrations, 36, 37 l bones, 40 inset saddle joint, 41 inset, 45 b, 48 bl, 57 tr, 76 inset, 82 all else, 83 all else, 89 all other art, 90 r, 93 inset artwork; U.S. National Library of Medicine: 22 l (Albrecht von Haller/C.J. Rollinus), 20, 21 (Charles Estienne/Étienne de la Rivière); Visuals Unlimited: 48 t (Donald Fawcett), 37 r spine (Ralph Hutchings), 64 (Richard Kessel); Wikipedia: 92 umami (Amtsga), 91 lct (Angelo Ruffini), 14 ctr (Benjah-bmm27), 40 ellipsoidal joint, 40 saddle joint (Brian C. Goss), 16 platelets (BruceBlaus), 87 octopus (Comingio Merculiano in Jatta Giuseppe), 88 tc, 89 brain art (Dgg32), 101 cr (fir0002/flagstaffotos.com.au), 22 cb (Hablot Knight Browne), 32 t bg, 33 t bg (Harald Hoyer), 88 cb, 89 kidneys art (LadyofHats), 14 cl, 31 t (OpenStax College, "Anatomy & Physiology," Connexions, June 19, 2013, http://cnx.org/content/col11496/1.6/), 101 c (Pueri Michał Klimont), 53 cl, 65 b (Rogeriopfm), 22 rtl (Stewart Mcfadyen), 101 cl (Velela), 91 lcb (Wbensmith), 23 ltl (Wilhelm Röntgen/NASA).

Credits and acknowledgments